CONTEMPORARY EUROPEAN ARCHITECTS

Rob Story
9/94
Frankfurt

CONTEMPORARY

Wolfgang Amsoneit

EUROPEAN ARCHITECTS

Benedikt Taschen

Page 2: Jean Nouvel, Mediapark Tower in Cologne, project 1990

© 1994 Benedikt Taschen Verlag GmbH
Hohenzollernring 53, D–50672 Köln
Edited by Rolf Taschen
Layout: Peter Gössel, Gabriele Leuthäuser, Nuremberg
Cover design: Angelika Muthesius, Cologne
English translation: Karen Williams, London
French translation: Marie-Anne Trémeau-Böhm, Cologne
Typesetting: Utesch Satztechnik GmbH, Hamburg
Reproductions: NUREG, Nuremberg
Printed by Graficas Estella, S.A.

Printed in Spain
ISBN 3-8228-9753-1

CONTENTS

Ivan Leonidov, Ministry of Heavy Industry in Red Square in Moscow, USSR, competition entry of 1933

The word at the end of the eighties was that »Post-Modernism« was dead. »Deconstruction« was now the latest trend. Is it still? What do Post-Modernism and deconstruction actually mean? And in which direction is architecture moving today? To venture a look into the future, we must first take a brief look at the past, back to the beginnings of Modernism.

Artists and architects at the end of the nineteenth century were confronted with the profound implications of the concept of mathematical abstraction in engineering. Art reacted to the principle of abstraction in physics with its own gradual renunciation of the object. It had no further use for the conjuring tricks which had previously produced richly decorative styles of architecture. It was here, at some mysterious hour, that the Modern Movement was born. Architecture began a shift towards pure form which, in the International Style of the twenties and thirties, was to become an aesthetic canon. Of profound significance for the history of architectural theory was the attempt by Henry-Russell Hitchcock and Philip Johnson, in 1931, to define the peculiar characteristics of the International Style. They identified its three main aesthetic principles as the emphasis upon pure volume, modular regularity, and the absence of wilful decoration. Modernism was equally preoccupied with the principle of freedom, which led to an individualization of architecture and to the end of the standardized type. It had previously been the type which, until well into the nineteenth century, had dictated both the building task and its solution.

In the wake of political revolution in the Soviet Union there emerged a Marxist art movement in which modernist architecture reached its peak. Russian architects of the twenties – El Lissitzky, Ivan Leonidov – explored the principles of space and construction with a sense of boundless possibilities in visionary designs. And although the experimental designs remained for the most part aesthetic utopias, they have continued to inspire architects right up to our own times.

After the Second World War and the destruction of much of Central Europe's legacy of historical architecture, the Modern Movement – temporarily under neo-classical pressure – returned to the scene with some new examples of the functional urban design which had been initiated in the 1933 Athens Charter. But the reductionist style of architecture which developed in the euphoria of post-war modernity had spent its force by the end of the seventies. After an odyssey through the world of limited possibilities it ended in stereotype, and was finally met with scepticism and resistance.

The history of style in the twentieth century is one of the modern versus the traditional. Post-Modernism,

Ende der achtziger Jahre hieß es, die »Postmoderne« sei tot. Aktuell sei die »Dekonstruktion«. Ist sie es noch? Was bedeutet überhaupt Postmoderne, was Dekonstruktion? Und in welche Richtung bewegt sich die Architektur? Um einen Blick in die Zukunft zu wagen, müssen wir einen kurzen Blick in die Vergangenheit werfen: auf den Beginn der Moderne.

Künstler und Architekten begegnen Ende des 19. Jahrhunderts den unübersehbaren Auswirkungen des Prinzips der mathematisch-physikalischen Abstraktion in den Ingenieurwissenschaften. Die Reaktion in der Kunst auf das Prinzip Abstraktion in der Physik ist ihr Weg zur Gegenstandslosigkeit. Für die Zauberformeln, die den dekorreichen Architekturstilen zugrunde liegen, gibt es keine Verwendung mehr. Dies ist, ohne eine genaue Zeit anzugeben, die Geburtsstunde der Moderne. In der Architektur entwickelt sich ein Purismus der reinen Form, der in den zwanziger und dreißiger Jahren – im International Style – zur ästhetischen Richtschnur wird. 1932 unternahmen Henry-Russell Hitchcock und Philip Johnson den theoriegeschichtlich bedeutenden Versuch, die besonderen Merkmale des International Style auf den Begriff zu bringen. Als die drei wichtigsten ästhetischen Prinzipien galten ihnen die Betonung reiner Volumen, modulare Regelmäßigkeit und die Vermeidung aufgesetzter Dekorationen. Ein weiterer wichtiger Gedanke der Moderne war das Prinzip Freiheit, das zu einer Individualisierung der Architektur und zum Ende des Typus führte. Der Typus hatte bis ins 19. Jahrhundert die Bauaufgabe und das Schema ihrer Lösung zugleich festgelegt.

In der Sowjetunion entwickelte sich im Zuge der politischen Revolution eine marxistische Kunstbewegung, in der die Architektur der Moderne zur Hochform gelangt. Russische Entwerfer der zwanziger Jahre, wie El Lissitzky und Iwan Leonidow, erforschten in visionären Entwürfen und einem Bewußtsein unbegrenzter Möglichkeiten die Prinzipien von Raum und Konstruktion. Die experimentellen Entwürfe blieben zum großen Teil ästhetisch-utopische Visionen. Aber bis heute noch zehren Generationen von Architekten davon.

Nach dem Zweiten Weltkrieg und der gewaltigen Zerstörung historischer Bausubstanz in Mitteleuropa tritt die Moderne, die vorübergehend unter neoklassizistischen Druck geraten war, mit neuen Leitbildern eines funktionellen Städtebaus auf den Plan, der 1933 in der Charta von Athen seinen Ausgangspunkt hatte. In der euphorischen Stimmung der Nachkriegsmoderne entwickelt sich eine reduzierte Architektur, die Ende der siebziger Jahre ihre Kraft verbraucht hat. Nach einer Odyssee durch die Welt begrenzter Möglichkeiten endet sie in Stereotypie und stößt schließlich auf Skepsis und Widerstand.

A la fin des années 80, on a dit que le »postmodernisme« était mort, que la »déconstruction« était actuelle. L'est-elle encore? Que signifie au juste postmodernisme, que signifie déconstruction? Et dans quelle direction l'architecture évolue-t-elle? Pour risquer un regard sur l'avenir, il nous faut jeter un coup d'œil sur le passé: sur le début du modernisme.

A la fin du XIXe siècle, les artistes et les architectes font face aux effets imprévisibles du principe de l'abstraction mathématico-physique dans les sciences de l'ingénieur. La réaction dans l'art au »principe de l'abstraction dans la physique« est son chemin vers la nonfiguration. Il n'y a plus d'emploi pour les formules magiques qui sont à la base des styles architecturaux richement décorés. C'est, sans donner d'époque précise, la date de naissance de l'époque moderne. Un purisme de la forme, qui devient la règle esthétique dans les années 20 et 30 – dans le style international –, se développe en architecture. En 1932, Henry-Russell Hitchcock et Philip Johnson tentent une expérience capitale du point de vue histoire de la théorie, c'est-à-dire définir les caractéristiques du style international. Pour eux, les trois principes esthétiques essentiels consistaient à accentuer les volumes purs, à utiliser des modules réguliers et à éviter les décorations rapportées. Une autre grande idée du mouvement moderne était le principe de la liberté qui aboutit à une individualisation de l'architecture et à la fin du type. Jusqu'au XIXe siècle, le type avait déterminé la construction et, en même temps, le schéma de sa réalisation.

En Union soviétique, une tendance artistique marxiste, dans laquelle l'architecture moderniste atteint son apogée, se développa au cours de la révolution politique. Des projeteurs des années 20 tels que El Lissitzky et Ivan Leonidov examinèrent les principes de l'espace et de la construction dans des projets visionnaires, conscients des possibilités illimitées. Les projets expérimentaux restèrent en grande partie des visions esthétiques utopiques. Mais aujourd'hui encore, des générations d'architectes en vivent.

Après la Deuxième Guerre mondiale et la destruction d'immenses volumes bâtis historiques en Europe centrale, le mouvement moderne, qui avait été pour un temps soumis à la pression du néo-classicisme, fit son apparition avec de nouveaux idéaux d'urbanisme fonctionnel dont le point de départ était la Charte d'Athènes de 1933. Dans l'atmosphère euphorique du modernisme de l'après-guerre se développe une architecture réduite qui est à bout de forces à la fin des années 70. Après avoir effectué une odyssée dans le monde des possibilités limitées, elle prend fin dans la stéréotypie et se heurte finalement au scepticisme et à l'opposition.

Pavilions for the exposition »What a Wonderful World! Music Videos in Architecture« in Groningen, Netherlands, 1990, designed by Coop Himmelblau (opposite page above), Bernard Tschumi (opposite page below), Zaha Hadid (this page above) and Rem Koolhaas (below)

John Outram, pumping station in the
London Docklands, Great Britain,
1989–1990

prompted by functionalist dreariness and encour-
aged by political and cultural protest movements at
the start of the seventies, is just one of many »revival«
movements reflecting a rediscovery of emotional val-
ues and a need for history. From our present perspective, however, Post-Modernism can also be seen as
the manifestation of the Modern Movement's process
of self-definition, as an effect of Modernism's attempt
to extricate itself from crisis by means of the counter-
innovations of history and ornament. Its architects
investigated various stylistic periods in terms of their
possible re-use and thereby discovered classicism
and the methods of historicism. Their journey through
time finally led them, at the end of the eighties, back to
the sore point of all stylistic conflicts – classical Modernism.

This dialectic view of Modernism's coming-full-circle
is supported by the contemporary return to classical
Modernism. Deconstructivism, whose geometric confusion supplemented and replaced Post-Modernism
in the mid-eighties, appears in this light as a reprise of
Constructivism. In contrast to the revolutionary Russia
of the twenties, however, Deconstructivism opens up
rather more negative utopias. Rediscovered Modernism is turning in circles. While traditional architectural
styles obeyed the biological cycle of birth, maturity
and death, the Modern Movement claimed to have
arrived at a radically new stage of evolution: from
now on, architecture was to advance scientifically,
according to the principles of aesthetic reduction. No
one considered the fact that, once the most reduced
level of form had been reached, any further »advance« could only be achieved through variation.
Linear movement thus becomes a circle; in other
words, all attempts to go beyond Modernism simply
lead back to the starting point.

GERMANY

The Second World War left German architecture scar-
red both physically – through severe bomb damage –
and intellectually – through the taboos placed on its
own history. Under the National Socialists, the architecture of the Bauhaus – that byword of German
Modernism – had been suppressed as »degenerate«.
At the same time, however, the traditionalism em-
braced and »racially« abused by National Socialism
was now outlawed. Two competing branches of an
architectural generation were thus crippled, if not entirely destroyed, and the conditions for the development of post-war architecture were the worst conceiv-
able. While German architects played a leading role
in shaping the international face of architecture in the
twenties and thirties, this was no longer true after the
war. Even such architects as Hans Scharoun, Egon

Die Stilgeschichte des 20. Jahrhunderts zeigt ein wechselvolles Ringen der Moderne mit dem Traditionalismus. Die durch funktionalistische Öde provozierte und durch politische und kulturelle Protestbewegungen Anfang der siebziger Jahre ausgelöste Postmoderne in der Architektur ist nur eine unter anderen »Umkehr-Bewegungen«, in denen sich eine Wiederentdeckung der Gefühlswerte und ein Bedürfnis nach Geschichte manifestiert. Aus heutiger Sicht läßt sich die Postmoderne allerdings auch als immanente Erscheinung des krisenhaften Selbstdefinitionsprozesses der Moderne erklären: als Münchhausen-Effekt des Versuchs der Moderne, sich am eigenen Schopfe aus der Krise zu ziehen – durch die Gegeninnovation Geschichte und Ornament. Die Architekten prüfen verschiedene Stilperioden auf ihre mögliche Wiederverwendung, entdecken dabei den Klassizismus und die Methode des Historismus. Schließlich führt sie ihre Zeitreise, Ende der achtziger Jahre, zum neuralgischen Punkt aller Stilkonflikte: zur klassischen Moderne.

Die aktuelle Rückeroberung der klassischen Moderne spricht für eine solche dialektische Sicht des Zu-sich-selber-Kommens der Moderne. Der Dekonstruktivismus, der die Postmoderne als Suchbewegung Mitte der achtziger Jahre – durch eine Verwirrung der Geometrie – ergänzt und die Architekturdiskussion der letzten Jahre bestimmt hat, erscheint in dieser Sicht als eine Reprise des Konstruktivismus. Anders jedoch als im revolutionären Rußland der zwanziger Jahre eröffnet der Dekonstruktivismus eher eine negative Utopie. Die wiedergefundene Moderne dreht sich im Kreis. Während sich die traditionellen Architekturstile nach dem Muster biologischer Prozesse – Geburt, Reife und Tod – entwickelten, nahm die Moderne für sich in Anspruch, zu einem radikal neuen Entwicklungstyp gekommen zu sein: Ab jetzt sollte der Fortschritt der Architektur wissenschaftlich, durch das Prinzip ästhetischer Reduktion, vorangetrieben werden. Daß man jedoch – einmal bei der reduziertesten Form angekommen – nur noch durch Variation würde »fortschreiten« können, hatte man nicht bedacht. Aus der linearen Bewegung wird ein Kreis, oder anders: Jeder Versuch, über die Moderne hinauszugehen, führt zu derselben zurück.

DEUTSCHLAND

Durch den Zweiten Weltkrieg hat die deutsche Architektur doppelt gelitten: physisch – durch die Zerstörungen der Bomben – und intellektuell – durch die Tabuisierung der eigenen Geschichte. In nationalsozialistischer Zeit wurde die Architektur des Bauhauses – Inbegriff der deutschen Moderne – als »entartet« unterdrückt. Gleichzeitig aber wurde der nationalso-

L'histoire des styles du XXe siècle témoigne d'une lutte mouvementée entre le modernisme et le traditionalisme. Le postmodernisme provoqué en architecture par la monotonie fonctionnaliste et les mouvements de protestation politiques et culturels du début des années 70 n'est qu'un »mouvement renversé« parmi d'autres, et où se manifeste une redécouverte des valeurs affectives et un besoin d'histoire. Du point de vue actuel, le postmodernisme se laisse toutefois aussi expliquer en tant que phénomène immanent du processus d'autodéfinition en crise du modernisme pour se sortir de la crise – par la contre-innovation histoire et ornement. Les architectes examinent diverses périodes stylistiques en ce qui concerne leur réemploi potentiel et découvrent à cette occasion le néo-classicisme et la méthode de l'historisme. Finalement, leur voyage dans le temps les conduit à la fin des années 80 au point neuralgique de tous les conflits stylistiques: le modernisme classique.

L'actuelle reconquête du modernisme classique parle en faveur d'un tel point de vue dialectique de l'éveil du modernisme. Le déconstructivisme, qui complète le postmodernisme en tant que mouvement de recherches au milieu des années 80 – par une confusion géométrique – et a déterminé la discussion architecturale des dernières années, apparaît sous cet angle comme une reprise du constructivisme. Toutefois, à la différence de la Russie révolutionnaire des années 20, le déconstructivisme inaugure plutôt une utopie négative. Le modernisme retrouvé tourne en rond. Alors que les styles architecturaux traditionnels se développaient sur le modèle des processus biologiques – naissance, maturité et mort –, le modernisme prétendit être parvenu à un type de développement radicalement nouveau: désormais, le progrès de l'architecture devait être activé scientifiquement par le principe de la réduction esthétique. On n'avait toutefois pas songé qu'une fois parvenu à la forme la plus réduite, on ne pourrait plus »progresser« que par la variation. Le mouvement linéaire se transforme en cercle, ou encore: toute tentative pour aller au-delà du modernisme y ramène.

ALLEMAGNE

A cause de la Deuxième Guerre mondiale, l'architecture allemande a doublement souffert: physiquement – par les destructions des bombes – et intellectuellement – en tabouisant sa propre histoire. A l'époque nazie, l'architecture du Bauhaus – incarnation du modernisme allemand – fut réprimée en tant qu'»art dégénéré«. Mais en même temps, le traditionalisme occupé par le nazisme, »nationalement« profané devint tabou, de sorte que deux lignes d'une génération d'architectes concurrents furent handicapées, sinon

Eiermann, Dominikus Böhm and Rudolf Schwarz had little influence abroad. The situation has barely changed today. It is every man for himself as the nation's leading architects fight for influence and for personal niches of self-fulfilment. The loyalty and consensus which might lend the architectural profession political clout are lacking. This state of isolationism is not exclusive to Germany, however.

At the peak of late-functionalist directionlessness in the seventies, confusion amongst the patrons of architecture seemed absolute. Investors sought refuge in profit-oriented building methods and site exploitation, authorities in the pointless perfectioning of planning laws, and architects in a pragmatic ethic which, in the words of Meinhard von Gerkan, has led to a »social pecking order of architectural styles«.

With regards to international architectural trends, Germany saw the arrival of Post-Modernism at the end of the seventies. Its impact was clearly reflected in the International Bauausstellung (IBA) in Berlin. In this exhibition of modern architecture, ongoing from 1984 to 1989 and directed by Josef Paul Kleihues, international celebrities were invited to come and build in Berlin. German architects were thereby left, initially at least, on the sidelines. With its first architecture exhibition in the Hansa district in 1956 and its works by Egon Eiermann and Hans Scharoun, Berlin had already demonstrated its special position in the field of architectural innovation. It has been a centre of vital stimuli for German architecture ever since. Prompted by the IBA exhibition, architecture has recently been rediscovered as a publicity medium for politics and industry. In Frankfurt, in particular, specific commissions awarded to internationally-renowned architects have created a successful counterbalance to the ruin of the city in the seventies. Oswald Mathias Ungers built the German Architectural Museum on the banks of the Main (1980), Richard Meier the Arts and Crafts Museum (1984), Günter Behnisch the Postmuseum (1990). Gustav Peichl and Hans Hollein are also represented in new museum buildings. In 1990 the German-American Helmut Jahn completed a new multi-storey trade fair building next to Ungers' Fair Gate House.

The German architectural scene at the start of the nineties reveals strong leanings towards reawakened classical Modernism. Three main trends can be identified:

a rational architecture whose aesthetic is governed by urban-planning considerations and which contains elements of classical Modernism. Its designs are largely theory-based and tend towards the typological. It is related to Italian Rationalism, which has its roots in the thirties. Leading practitioners in this field

Meinhard von Gerkan, Volkwin Mang, Jörg Schlaich, glass roof over the inner courtyard of the History of Hamburg Museum, Germany, 1989

zialistisch okkupierte, »völkisch« mißbrauchte Traditionalismus zum Tabu, so daß zwei Linien einer konkurrierenden Architektengeneration behindert, wenn nicht gar ausgeschaltet wurden: Die Entwicklung der Nachkriegsarchitektur hatte die denkbar schlechtesten Voraussetzungen. Während das internationale Architekturschaffen in den zwanziger und dreißiger Jahren entscheidend von deutschen Architekten mitgeprägt wurde, konnte davon nach dem Kriege nicht mehr die Rede sein. Selbst Architekten wie Hans Scharoun, Egon Eiermann, Dominikus Böhm und Rudolf Schwarz gewannen im Ausland wenig Einfluß. In diesem Punkt hat sich die Situation der deutschen Architektur nur wenig verändert. Die tonangebenden Architekten kämpfen – jeder für sich – um Einfluß und suchen nach Nischen persönlicher Selbstverwirlichung. Es mangelt an Loyalität und Konsens, die der Architektenschaft urbanistisch-politisches Gewicht verleihen könnten. Doch dieser Zustand der Isolierung ist auch in anderen Ländern zu beobachten.

Auf dem Höhepunkt der spätfunktionalistischen Orientierungslosigkeit in den siebziger Jahren schien der Dissens der Architekturträger perfekt. Die Investoren suchten ihr Heil in gewinnorientierten Bauweisen und Grundstücksausnutzungen, die Behörden in sinnloser Perfektionierung des Planungsrechts und die Architekten in einer pragmatischen Architekturethik, die – wie Meinhard von Gerkan beschreibt – zu einer »gesellschaftlichen Hackordnung der Architekturstile« geführt hat.

Mit Blick auf die internationalen Architekturströmungen hielt Ende der siebziger Jahre auch in Deutschland die Postmoderne Einzug. Sichtbare Auswirkungen hatte dies insbesondere bei der Internationalen Bauausstellung (IBA) in Berlin unter der Führung von Josef Paul Kleihues in der Zeit von 1984 bis 1989. Wer international Rang und Namen hatte, wurde zum Bauen in Berlin aufgefordert, wobei deutsche Architekten zunächst in einer Zuschauerrolle verharrten. Schon mit der ersten Bauausstellung im Hansaviertel 1956 mit den Arbeiten von Egon Eiermann und Hans Scharoun hatte Berlin seine architekturinnovative Sonderstellung demonstriert. Seit dieser Zeit gehen entscheidende Impulse für deutsche Architekturentwicklungen von Berlin aus. Ausgelöst durch die IBA, wurde die Architektur in den letzten Jahren als Werbeträger von Politik und Industrie wiederentdeckt. Besonders in Frankfurt gelang es, der in den siebziger Jahren zerstörten Stadtlandschaft durch gezielte Bauaufträge an international bedeutende Architekten ein architektonisches Gegengewicht zu verleihen. Oswald Mathias Ungers baute am Mainufer das Deutsche Architekturmuseum (1980), Richard Meier das Museum für Kunsthandwerk (1984), Günter Behnisch

éliminées: le développement de l'architecture de l'après-guerre avait les conditions les plus mauvaises que l'on puisse s'imaginer. Tandis que la création architecturale internationale des années 20 et 30 était décisivement marquée par des architectes allemands, il ne pouvait plus en être question après la guerre. Même des architectes tels que Hans Scharoun, Egon Eiermann, Dominikus Böhm et Rudolf Schwarz prirent peu d'influence sur l'étranger. Sur ce point, la situation de l'architecture allemande n'a guère changé. Les architectes qui donnent le ton luttent – chacun pour soi – pour acquérir de l'influence et cherchent des créneaux d'autoréalisation personnelle. La loyauté et le consensus, qui pourraient donner aux architectes un poids urbanistique et politique, manquent. Mais cet isolement peut également être observé dans d'autres pays.

Au sommet du manque d'orientation fonctionnaliste tardif dans les années 70, le désaccord des protagonistes de l'architecture semblait parfait. Les investisseurs cherchaient leur salut dans des méthodes de construction et des exploitations immobilières orientées vers le profit, les administrations dans le perfectionnement absurde de la législation en matière de planification et les architectes dans une éthique architecturale pragmatique qui a abouti – comme le rapporte Meinhard von Gerkan – à une »hiérarchie des styles architecturaux«.

Face aux courants architecturaux internationaux, le postmodernisme fit aussi son entrée en Allemagne à la fin des années 70. Ceci eut des répercussions visibles, en particulier lors de l'IBA (exposition internationale de la construction) à Berlin sous la direction de Josef Paul Kleihues, entre 1984 et 1989. Les architectes ayant une position et un nom connus à l'échelon international furent invités à construire à Berlin, à l'occasion de quoi les architectes allemands se cantonnèrent d'abord dans un rôle de spectateur. Avec la première exposition de la construction dans le quartier Hansa en 1956 et avec les travaux de Egon Eiermann et de Hans Scharoun, Berlin avait déjà démontré sa position spéciale innovatrice en matière d'architecture. Depuis cette époque, Berlin donne des impulsions décisives pour l'évolution de l'architecture allemande. Par suite de l'IBA, l'architecture a été redécouverte en tant que support publicitaire par la politique et l'industrie au cours des dernières années. A Francfort surtout, on est parvenu à redonner au paysage urbain ravagé dans les années 70 un contrepoids architectonique en passant des commandes à des architectes de renommée internationale. Oswald Mathias Ungers a construit le Musée allemand de l'architecture au bord du Main (1980), Richard Meier le Musée des arts artisanaux (1984), Günter Behnisch

Heinz Bienefeld, Villa Heinze in
Cologne, Germany, 1984–1988

include Oswald M. Ungers, Josef P. Kleihues, Hans. F.
Kollhoff, the Dietrich Bangert group with Bernd Jansen, Laurids Ortner etc.;

a new Expressionism: a sculptural architecture combining traditional and modern elements, as also
found on the contemporary Spanish architectural
scene. This trend is strongly influenced by the buildings of Dominikus Böhm (1880–1955) and is pur-
veyed by Gottfried Böhm, Heinz Bienefeld, Karl-Josef
Schattner, Rolf Link etc.;

a neo-modernist architecture which takes technical
building components as the starting-point for its design initiatives. As the largest and most influential of
the three groups, it included such architects as Günter
Behnisch, Joachim Schürmann, Erich Schneider-
Wessling, Otto Steidle etc. Another variety of neo-
modernism is deconstructivism.

Ungers, with his drawings and theories, rose to become a central figure in the German architectural
debate at the end of the seventies. His early works of
the fifties had already earned him an international
reputation. His withdrawal into university life in Berlin
and New York in the sixties was a period of fruitful
theoretical development in drawings and philosophies of form. As a teacher he exerted a strong
influence on the younger architect generation. Ungers
seeks to introduce a metaphysical dimension into
Modernism by means of Surrealism. The metaphysics
of space and time in the spirit of Giorgio de Chirico's
»pittura metafisica«, and the history of architectural
ideas, are his chief objectives for a new ethic of Modernism. In 1991 Ungers proposed such a recourse to
history for the architectural project »Berlin morgen« in
the Deutsches Architekturmuseum, namely in the
realization of important buildings of classical Modernism – a means, too, of breaking out of the vicious
circle of compulsive innovation at all costs. With his
understanding of architecture Ungers links theory and
practice, the past, present and future of architecture. It
is this which explains his silent leadership of the German architectural scene.

The traditionalism of Cologne ecclesiastical architect
Dominikus Böhm has its roots in German Expressionism, whose preferred idioms have always been
monumentality and poetry. Heinz Bienefeld, a pupil of
Dominikus Böhm, has created a significant body of
small buildings over the last thirty years of his career
which have gained greater recognition abroad than
at home. Through the rather chance history of his
clientele, he has become one of the most important
villa architects in Central Europe. In his designs he
works out the typological and symbolical elements of
the detached villa and arrives at a precise definition of
his architecture. His typological rigour is matched by

das Postmuseum (1990). Auch Gustav Peichl und Hans Hollein sind mit ganz neuen Museumsbauten vertreten. 1990 realisiert der Deutschamerikaner Helmut Jahn ein neues Messehochhaus neben dem Torhaus von Ungers.

Anfang der neunziger Jahre stellt sich die deutsche Architekturszene mit starken Tendenzen zur wiedererwachten klassischen Moderne dar. Drei Hauptströmungen sind zu erkennen:

eine rationale Architektur mit einer präzisen städtebaulich geleiteten Ästhetik und Elementen der klassischen Moderne. Der Entwurfsansatz ist wesentlich theoriegestützt und tendiert zum Typologischen. Es besteht eine Verwandtschaft zum italienischen Rationalismus, der seine Wurzeln in den dreißiger Jahren hat. Hauptvertreter dieser Richtung sind Ungers, Kleihues, Hans F. Kollhoff, die Gruppe Dietrich Bangert, Bernd Jansen, Laurids Ortner u. a.;

ein neuer Expressionismus: eine bildhauerisch-sinnliche Architektur mit einer Verbindung von traditionellen und modernen Elementen, wie sie auch in der aktuellen spanischen Architekturszene zu beobachten ist. Diese Richtung ist stark von der Architektur Dominikus Böhms (1880–1955) geprägt. Hauptvertreter sind Gottfried Böhm, Heinz Bienefeld, Karl-Josef Schattner, Rolf Link u. a.;

eine neomoderne Architektur mit technisch-konstruktiven Elementen als Ausgangspunkt ihrer Gestaltungsansätze. Diese Richtung bildet die zahlenmäßig stärkste und im Wettbewerb einflußreichste Gruppe mit Architekten wie Günter Behnisch, Joachim Schürmann, Erich Schneider-Wessling, Otto Steidle u. a. Eine weitere Spielart der Neomoderne ist der Dekonstruktivismus.

Ungers wurde Ende der siebziger Jahre mit seinen Zeichnungen und Theorien zur Zentralfigur in der deutschen Architekturdiskussion. Schon mit seinen frühen Arbeiten der fünfziger Jahre wurde er international bekannt. Sein Rückzug an die Hochschule in Berlin und New York in den sechziger Jahren führte zu einer fruchtbaren theoretischen Auseinandersetzung durch Zeichnungen und Philosophien zur Formfindung. Als Architekturlehrer gewann er großen Einfluß auf die nachfolgende Architektengeneration. Ungers versucht, der Moderne über den Surrealismus eine metaphysische Dimension zu eröffnen. Die Metaphysik von Raum und Zeit im Sinne von Giorgio de Chiricos »Pittura metafisica« und eine Ideengeschichte der Architektur sind seine Hauptanliegen für eine neue Ethik der Moderne. 1991 schlägt Ungers einen solchen Rekurs auf die Ideengeschichte für das Architekturprojekt »Berlin morgen« des Deutschen Architekturmuseums vor: die Realisierung bedeutender Bauten der klassischen Moderne – auch um den Teufels-

le Musée postal (1990). Gustav Peichl et Hans Hollein sont également représentés par de nouveaux musées. En 1990, l'Américain d'origine allemande Helmut Jahn a réalisé une nouvelle tour des foires à côté de la maison-porche de Ungers.

Au début des années 90, la scène architecturale allemande présente de fortes tendances au modernisme classique renaissant. On distingue trois tendances principales:

une architecture rationnelle avec une esthétique précise guidée par l'urbanisme, et des éléments du modernisme classique. L'idée du projet est en grande partie soutenue par la théorie et tend à la typologie. Il y a une parenté avec le rationalisme italien qui a son origine dans les années 30. Les principaux représentants de cette tendance sont Ungers, Kleihues, Hans F. Kollhoff, le groupe Dietrich Bangert, Bernd Jansen, Laurids Ortner, etc.;

un nouvel expressionnisme: une architecture plastique sensible avec une combinaison d'éléments traditionnels et modernes que l'on peut également observer sur la scène architecturale espagnole actuelle. Cette tendance est fortement marquée par l'architecture de Dominikus Böhm (1880–1955). Ses principaux représentants sont Gottfried Böhm, Heinz Bienefeld, Karl Josef Schattner, Rolf Link, etc.;

une architecture néo-moderne avec des éléments techniques constructifs comme point de départ de ses créations. Cette tendance constitue le groupe le plus important en nombre et le plus influent dans les concours avec des architectes tels que Günter Behnisch, Joachim Schürmann, Erich Schneider-Wessling, Otto Steidle, etc. Le déconstructivisme constitue une autre variante du néo-modernisme.

A la fin des années 70, Ungers est devenu, avec ses dessins et ses théories, le personnage central de la discussion architecturale allemande. Il est parvenu à la célébrité internationale avec ses œuvres du début des années 50. Le fait qu'il se soit retiré à l'université à Berlin et à New York dans les années 60 a abouti à une discussion théorique féconde par suite de dessins et de philosophies ayant trait à la forme. En tant que professeur d'architecture, il a acquis une grande influence sur la génération suivante. Ungers essaie d'ouvrir une dimension métaphysique au mouvement moderne en passant par le surréalisme. La métaphysique de l'espace et du temps au sens de la »Pittura metafisica« de Giorgio de Chirico et une histoire des idées de l'architecture sont ses principales préoccupations pour parvenir à une nouvelle éthique du modernisme. En 1991, Ungers propose un tel recours à l'histoire des idées pour le projet architectural »Berlin morgen« (Berlin demain) du Musée allemand de l'architecture: la réalisation d'importantes constructions

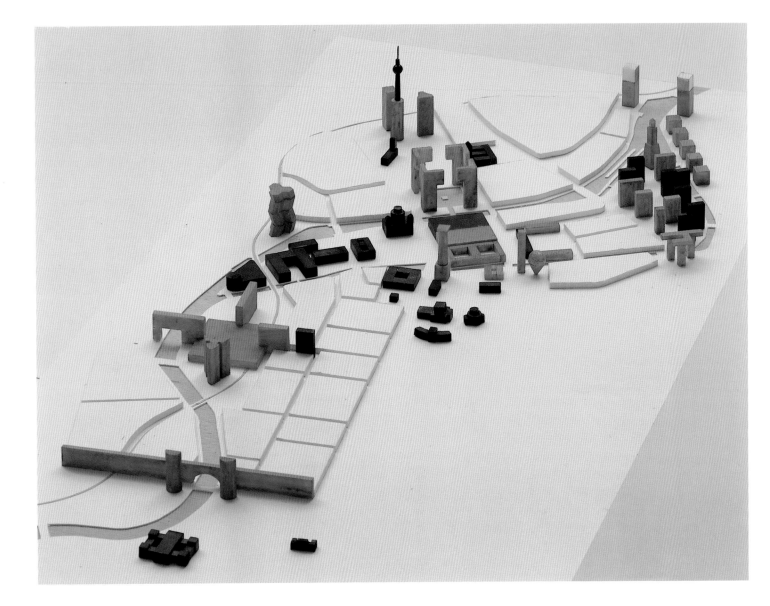

Oswald Mathias Ungers, entry for the
»Berlin morgen« exhibition in the
Deutsches Architekturmuseum, 1991

the precision with which he designs doors, windows, bathrooms and roof trusses. The complexity of his details approaches the level of the Italian Carlo Scarpa. His designs are developed in orthogonal projections such as are employed in mechanical engineering. This emphatic modelling of visible components is both a design philosophy and a pointed criticism of the serial nature of our modern construction methods as dictated by the building industry and excessive technical specifications. Through his practical work as an architect Bienefeld calls for a renewal of architecture and urban planning. In his opinion, a city model should be available in every European metropolis as a visual working aid for architects and politicians.

Gottfried Böhm received his basic architectural education from his father Dominikus. His training as a sculptor is reflected in the expressive plasticity of his works. His sensuous understanding of architecture emerges in numerous churches built since the mid-fifties. Even during the seventies era of raw functional-

kreis einer zwanghaften »Innovation um jeden Preis« zu durchbrechen. Mit seiner Architekturauffassung schlägt Ungers eine Brücke zwischen Theorie und Praxis, zwischen Vergangenheit, Gegenwart und Zukunft der Architektur. Darin ist seine heimliche Führerschaft in der deutschen Architekturszene begründet.

Die Traditionalismuslinie des Kölner Kirchenbaumeisters Dominikus Böhm hat ihre Wurzeln im deutschen Expressionismus. Monumentalität und Poesie waren seit je die bevorzugten Ausdrucksmöglichkeiten dieser Stilrichtung. Heinz Bienefeld, ein Meisterschüler Böhms, hat in den letzten dreißig Jahren seines Schaffens ein bedeutendes Œuvre kleiner Bauten realisiert, die international mehr Beachtung gefunden haben als in Deutschland. Durch die eher zufällige Geschichte seiner Klientel ist er zu einem der bedeutendsten Villenarchitekten Mitteleuropas geworden. In seinen Entwürfen arbeitet er das Typologische und Symbolische der freistehenden Villa heraus und gelangt mit entschlossenem Formwillen zur präzisen gestalterischen Definition seiner Architektur. Neben der typologischen Schärfe überrascht die Genauigkeit, mit der er Türanlagen, Fenster, Bäder und Dachstühle durchbildet. Die Komplexität seiner Details erreicht das Niveau des Italieners Carlo Scarpa. Die Methode seiner Entwurfsarbeit ist gekennzeichnet durch das Entwikkeln der Details in orthogonalen Projektionen, ähnlich wie im Maschinenbau. In dieser starken Überformung sichtbarer Bauteile steckt eine Entwurfsphilosophie und zugleich eine entschiedene Kritik an dem seriellen Charakter unserer Bauweisen unter dem Diktat der Bauindustrie und übertriebener technischer Vorschriften. Aus seiner praktischen Arbeit als Architekt zieht Bienefeld die Forderung nach einer Erneuerung der Baukunst und der Stadtbaukunst. Nach seiner Idee sollte in jeder europäischen Großstadt ein Stadtmodell als sinnliche Arbeitshilfe für Architekten und Politiker zur Verfügung stehen.

Gottfried Böhm erhielt seine Grundausbildung bei seinem Vater Dominikus. Seine Ausbildung als Bildhauer hat in der expressiven und plastischen Formung seiner Arbeiten Niederschlag gefunden. Seine sinnliche Architekturauffassung wird in zahlreichen Kirchenbauten seit Mitte der fünfziger Jahre deutlich. Böhm hat auch in der Phase des rüden Funktionalismus in den siebziger Jahren seine Architektur als Gesamtkunstwerk vorgetragen. Lange bevor in der Architekturtheorie der Kontextualismus zum Thema wurde, hat er seine Bauten kunstvoll auf die Landschaft bezogen und in die jeweilige historische Umgebung eingefügt. Ähnlich wie im Spätwerk seines Vaters vollzog sich auch bei ihm ein stilistischer Wandel. Böhm verließ in den achtziger Jahren sein expressives Formenvokabular und entwarf bei verschiedenen

du modernisme classique – également pour briser le cercle vicieux d'une »innovation à tout prix« contrainte. Avec sa conception de l'architecture, Ungers lance un pont entre la théorie et la pratique, entre le passé, le présent et l'avenir de l'architecture. C'est là le fondement de son leadership secret sur la scène architecturale allemande.

La ligne du traditionalisme du bâtisseur d'églises colonais Dominikus Böhm a son origine dans l'expressionnisme allemand. La monumentalité et la poésie ont toujours été les moyens d'expression préférés de cette tendance stylistique. Heinz Bienefeld, un élève de Dominikus Böhm, a réalisé au cours des 30 dernières années de remarquables petites constructions qui ont plus attiré l'attention dans le monde qu'en Allemagne. De par l'histoire plutôt accidentelle de sa clientèle, il est devenu l'un des plus grands constructeurs de villas d'Europe centrale. Dans ses projets, il fait ressortir le typologique et le symbolique de la villa isolée et parvient avec une intention formelle déterminée à une définition créatrice précise de son architecture. Outre la précision typologique, la minutie avec laquelle il développe ses portes, fenêtres, salles de bains et combles est surprenante. La complexité de ses détails atteint le niveau de l'Italien Carlo Scarpa. La méthode de son travail d'étude est caractérisée par le développement des détails dans des projections orthogonales, de même que dans la construction mécanique. Dans cette surconception d'éléments de construction visibles se trouve une philosophie d'étude et en même temps une critique résolue à l'égard du caractère sériel de nos méthodes de construction placées sous le diktat de l'industrie du bâtiment et de prescriptions techniques exagérées. Bienefeld tire de son travail pratique d'architecte la demande de renouvellement de l'architecture et de l'urbanisme. Selon lui, il devrait y avoir dans chaque grande ville européenne une maquette de la ville comme auxiliaire de travail sensible à la disposition des architectes et des politiciens.

Gottfried Böhm a reçu sa formation de base auprès de son père Dominikus. Sa formation de sculpteur se reflète dans la réalisation expressive et plastique de ses constructions. Sa conception sensible de l'architecture est distincte dans de nombreux édifices religieux construits depuis le milieu des années 50. Böhm a également exécuté son architecture comme œuvre d'art globale dans la phase du fonctionnalisme brut dans les années 70. Bien avant que le contextualisme ne devienne un thème de la théorie architecturale, il a artistement rapporté ses constructions au paysage et les a insérées dans leurs milieux historiques respectifs. Tout comme dans l'œuvre tardif de son père, il y a également eu un tournant stylistique chez lui. Dans les

Behnisch & Partner, Deutsches Postmuseum in Frankfurt/Main, Germany,
1990 (above)

Behnisch & Partner, University of Stuttgart Hysolar Research Institute, Germany, 1987 (opposite page)

ism, Böhm presented his architecture as a total work
of art. He was integrating his buildings into their
natural and historical environments long before contextualism became the subject of architectural theory.
Like his father in his late works, Gottfried too under-
went a radical stylistic change, abandoning his
expressive formal vocabulary in the eighties and developing, through a series of commissions, the architectural type of a three-aisled cathedral. The Züblinhaus in Stuttgart is particularly noteworthy in this
context. Böhm here removes the barriers between
sacred and profane architecture. Böhm's typology,
fully developed there, is always related in some way
to an urban context. Type and town are the central
reference variables in his works.

Since his stadium buildings for the 1972 Munich
Olympic Games, which he developed together with
Frei Otto, Stuttgart architect Günter Behnisch has
been acknowledged as one of the leading representatives of contemporary German modernism. His architecture derives a large part of its appeal from ex-

Bauaufgaben den Architekturtypus einer dreischiffigen Kathedrale. In dieser Werklinie ist besonders das Züblinhaus in Stuttgart zu nennen. Böhm leistet hier durch die Anwendung seines ausgeformten Typus die Aufhebung von sakraler und weltlicher Architektur. Die Typologie hat bei Böhm immer etwas mit einem städtebaulichen Kontext zu tun. Typus und Stadt sind die zentralen Bezugsgrößen in seinen Arbeiten.

Der Stuttgarter Architekt Günter Behnisch gilt mit dem Bau des Münchener Olympiastadions von 1972, das er gemeinsam mit Frei Otto entwickelte, als einer der führenden Vertreter der Moderne in Deutschland. Seine Architektur bezieht einen wesentlichen Teil ihres Reizes aus den ausdrucksstarken Details. Bereits die Formung eines Geländers ebenso wie das Design des Mobiliars wird zum wichtigen Architekturthema. Offensichtlich gelingt es Behnisch, die deutsche Designtradition der fünfziger Jahre fortzuführen, unter besonderer Bezugnahme auf die Möbelentwürfe des legendären Egon Eiermann. Die Dinge, so Behnisch, »sollen sich nach ihren eigenen Gesetzen ausfor-

années 80, Böhm a abandonné son vocabulaire formel expressif et a conçu dans diverses constructions le type architectural de cathédrale à trois nefs. Dans cette ligne, citons en particulier la Züblinhaus à Stuttgart. En employant son type étudié, Böhm parvient à abolir la distinction entre architecture sacrée et architecture profane. Chez Böhm, la typologie a toujours quelque chose à faire avec le contexte urbanistique. Le type et la ville sont les principales grandeurs de référence dans son œuvre.

Grâce à la construction du stade olympique de Munich en 1972, qu'il développa avec Frei Otto, l'architecte stuttgartien Günter Behnisch est considéré comme l'un des principaux représentants du modernisme en Allemagne. Son architecture tire une partie essentielle de son charme de détails expressifs. La réalisation d'une rampe et le design du mobilier deviennent déjà un important thème architectural. Apparemment, Behnisch parvient à continuer la tradition allemande du design des années 50 en se référant tout particulièrement aux projets de meubles du lé-

pressive details. Thus the modelling of a set of railings and the design of the furnishings may themselves become important architectural themes. Behnisch has clearly succeeded in perpetuating the German design tradition of the fifties, with particular reference to the furniture designs of the legendary Egon Eiermann. Things, according to Behnisch, »should shape themselves in obedience with their own laws«. The production and administrative buildings which he completed in collaboration with Andreas Theilig for the firm of Leybold-Heraeus in Alzenau occupy a prominent position amongst his late works. With the powerful expression achieved by its geometric form, its compositional clarity and the perfection of its details, the building approaches those of early Russian modernism. Behnisch's recently-opened Postmuseum on the museum embankment in Frankfurt reflects his continuing philosophy of open architecture, and undoubtedly ranks as one of the most interesting projects in German architecture today – even if the impact of this glass architectural machine is somewhat obscured by fashionable accessories. In his earlier Solar Institute in Stuttgart, Behnisch went a step further, venturing a bizarre collage in the new spirit of deconstruction. Self-critical and humorous at once, he describes it as a »late folly of youth«. Behnisch finds historical starting-points for his German deconstructivism in the corrugated-iron and cascade architecture of fifties Expressionism, which he consideres just as important as the architecture of the baroque, the revolutionary concepts of Russian Constructivism and the high school of Italian design. With this tendency towards bizarre architectural collage in more recent testimonials, Behnisch takes in deconstruction as a contemporary fashion and robs it of its critical function.

Germany is also home to an unusual form of »bioarchitecture«, which in part employs certain anthroposophic elements. From a historical point of view, it is the most successful and perhaps the most momentous product of the anti-establishment architecture of the seventies. Bio-architecture has come a long way from its »green« origins. Although a number of architects have now mastered the professional techniques of biological building, demand remains limited to a relatively small number of clients. The aesthetics of ecological architecture are not to everyone's taste. Nevertheless, current reserve is chiefly explained by the high costs of the building materials and energy-saving systems involved. It is not to be expected that bio-architecture will provide an early solution to the pressing need for mass housing at an economic price.

Germany, unlike its European neighbours, has severed the link between competition and architectural

Gottfried Böhm, Züblin Headquarters in Stuttgart, Germany, 1981–1984

men«. Einen bedeutenden Rang in Behnischs Spätwerk nimmt das Produktions- und Verwaltungsgebäude für die Firma Leybold-Heraeus in Alzenau ein, das er unter Mitwirkung von Andreas Theilig realisierte. Geometrischer Formwille, Ausdruckskraft der klaren Komposition und Perfektion des Details rücken dieses Bauwerk in die Nähe der frühen russischen Moderne. Behnischs offener Architekturauffassung entspricht auch sein kürzlich eröffnetes Postmuseum am Frankfurter Museumsufer. Es gehört sicherlich zu den interessantesten Projekten der aktuellen deutschen Architektur, auch wenn der Eindruck der gläsernen Architekturmaschine etwas unter modischen Zutaten leidet. Beim vorher gebauten Hysolar-Forschungsinstitut der Universität Stuttgart geht er noch einen Schritt weiter: Im neuen Trend der Dekonstruktion wagt Behnisch hier eine bizarre Collage. Selbstkritisch und humorvoll zugleich bezeichnet er dies als eine »späte Jungendsünde«. Historische Bezüge für seinen deutschen Dekonstruktivismus findet Behnisch in der Wellblech- und Kaskadenarchitektur des Fünfziger-Jahre-Expressionismus. Sie ist ihm ebenso wichtig wie die Barockarchitektur, die revolutionären Formideen des russischen Konstruktivismus und die hohe Schule des italienischen Designs. Mit seiner Neigung zur bizarren Architekturcollage in neueren Gutachten vereinnahmt Behnisch die Dekonstruktion als gängige Architekturmode und bringt sie um ihre architekturkritische Funktion.

Eine bemerkenswerte Facette stellt in Deutschland die »Bioarchitektur« dar, die zum Teil anthroposophische Elemente in sich aufgenommen hat. Sie ist — historisch gesehen — das erfolgreichste und vielleicht auch zukunftsträchtigste Ergebnis der Verweigerungsarchitektur der siebziger Jahre. Seit ihrem alternativen Anfang hat sich die Bioarchitektur inzwischen weit entwickelt. Obwohl einige Architekten inzwischen professionell die Methoden des biologischen Bauens beherrschen, bleibt die Nachfrage immer noch auf eine relativ kleine Zahl von Bauherren beschränkt. Die Ästhetik der Ökoarchitektur ist nicht jedermanns Sache. Der Hauptgrund für diese Zurückhaltung liegt aber in erster Linie an den hohen Kosten der Baustoffe und energiesparenden Systeme. Eine Antwort auf die drängenden Fragen des kostengünstigen Massenwohnungsbaus ist von der Bioarchitektur vorerst nicht zu erwarten.

Anders als in benachbarten europäischen Ländern ist das zahlenmäßig starke Wettbewerbswesen von der architekturgeschichtlichen Entwicklung abgekoppelt. Der Wettbewerb hat seine architekturkritische Filterfunktion verloren: Jeder Modebazillus graphisch neuartiger und abstrakter Strichcollagen begeistert ein Heer von Epigonen. Berlin bildet einen positiven

gendaire Egon Eiermann. Les choses, dit Behnisch, »doivent se former selon leurs propres lois«. Le bâtiment de production et d'administration de la firme Leybold-Heraeus à Alzenau, réalisé en collaboration avec Andreas Theilig, occupe une place essentielle dans l'œuvre tardif de Behnisch. Volonté de forme géométrique, force d'expression de la composition claire et perfection du détail rapprochent cet édifice du modernisme russe du début. A la conception architecturale ouverte de Behnisch correspond également son Musée postal récemment inauguré, qui fait certainement partie des projets les plus intéressants de l'architecture allemande contemporaine, même si l'impression de machine architectonique de verre souffre un peu des ingrédients à la mode. Dans l'Institut de recherche solaire de l'université de Stuttgart construit auparavant, il va encore plus loin. Dans la nouvelle tendance de la déconstruction, Behnisch ose ici un collage bizarre. A la fois autocritique et plein d'humour, il qualifie cela de »péché de jeunesse tardif«. Behnisch trouve des rapports historiques pour son déconstructivisme allemand dans l'architecture en tôle ondulée et en cascade de l'expressionnisme des années 50. A ses yeux, elle est tout aussi importante que l'architecture baroque, les idées formelles révolutionnaires du constructivisme russe et la haute école du design italien. Avec son penchant pour le collage architectural bizarre exprimé dans ses récentes expertises, Behnisch revendique la déconstruction en tant que mode architecturale courante et la prive de sa fonction critique.

La »bioarchitecture«, qui a partiellement repris des éléments anthroposophes, représente en Allemagne une facette remarquable. Du point de vue historique, elle est le résultat le plus brillant et peut-être aussi le plus prometteur de l'architecture de refus des années 70. Depuis son début alternatif, la bioarchitecture s'est grandement développée. Bien qu'entre-temps quelques architectes possèdent professionnellement les méthodes de construction biologiques, la demande est toujours limitée à un nombre de clients relativement petit. L'esthétique de l'architecture écologique n'est pas du goût de tout le monde. La principale raison de cette réserve tient avant tout aux coûts élevés des matériaux de construction et des systèmes sobres en énergie. Pour le moment, il ne faut pas s'attendre à ce que l'architecture biologique fournisse une réponse aux questions pressantes posées par la construction de grands ensembles à bas prix.

A la différence des pays européens voisins, le monde des concours, important en chiffres, n'est pas lié au développement de l'histoire de l'architecture. Le concours a perdu sa fonction de filtre dans le domaine de la critique de l'architecture: chaque mode

Jamie Troughton, John McAslan, Riverside Apartments, London, Great Britain, 1986–1990

development. Competition has lost its filtering, critical function for architecture. Every novel and abstract trend is now slavishly copied by a host of lesser imitators. Only Berlin offers a haven of equilibrium from the synchronized and tactical manoeuvring of the various currents of German competition. Finally, German architecture's lack of self-confidence is also reflected in its fear of an aesthetic of self-portrayal. Thus German architectural journals sooner resemble legal bulletins than the artistically bold publications found in Italy and Spain.

BRITAIN

In the mid-sixties, in the wake of Pop Art, there emerged a utopian, »arthropodal« vein of anti-establishment architecture which may be seen as a herald of deconstruction. Its protagonists came to include the Haus-Rucker-Co. group, active in Düsseldorf (dissolved 1991), Coop Himmelblau, and the London-based Archigram group with Peter Cook amongst its leaders. Archigram in particular was of decisive importance for the European architectural scene. In the technological euphoria of the seventies, its critical revelation of a super-futuristic fantasy world was positively construed by many architects, and led to a surge of experimental designs ranging from stackable containers to the perfected development of prefabricated-part systems. Two important English architects emerged from this High-Tech branch of architecture who were later to make Archigram ideas a reality – Richard Rogers and Norman Foster.

After initial collaboration with Foster, Rogers founded his own practice and pursued a more sculpturally expressive line of High-Tech architecture. He employed the formal language of the Archigram »Plug-in City« project (1964–1966) for the Centre Pompidou in Paris (1971–1977 with Renzo Piano) and again in the Lloyds Building in London (1982).

Norman Foster's works recall projects by Cedric Price, another English representative of »arthropodal« architecture. Price envisaged his Fun Palace (1961–1964) as an industrial megastructure with skin. This same idea lay behind Foster's design for the Willis Faber & Dumas insurance headquarters in Ipswich (1975). At a time when assertive architectural design was almost taboo, Foster developed in this building an aesthetic of the abstract, a return to the means of classical modernism. The glazing of its entire curved façade offered a new opportunity for abstraction and at the same time a miraculous escape from the aggressive physicality of seventies functionalism. His rediscovery of the glass curtain wall in the spirit of Mies van der Rohe's 1921 glass skyscraper, and his logical development of a new aesthetic of the supporting

Ruhepol in den angepaßten und taktischen Such-
manövern der deutschen Wettbewerbsströmungen.
Schließlich spiegelt sich das mangelnde Selbstbe-
wußtsein deutscher Architektur in der Angst vor dem
Prinzip Ästhetik wider. Deutsche Architektur-Fachzeit-
schriften ähneln eher juristischen Bulletins als gestalterisch avancierten Publikationen wie in Italien oder
Spanien.

ENGLAND

Mitte der sechziger Jahre, im Zuge der Pop Art, for-
mierte sich eine utopistische – »arthropodische« –
Verweigerungsarchitektur, die als Vorbereiter der Dekonstruktion gesehen werden kann. Zu den Haupt-
vertretern zählten wenige Jahre später die in Düsseldorf arbeitende österreichische Gruppe Haus-Ruk-
ker-Co (1991 aufgelöst), Coop Himmelblau und die
Londoner Gruppe Archigram mit ihrem Protagonisten
Peter Cook. Besonders von Archigram gingen entscheidende Impulse auf die europäische Architektur
aus. Die kritische Botschaft einer superfuturistischen
Scheinwelt wurde – in der technologischen Euphorie
der siebziger Jahre – von vielen Architekten affirmativ
gedeutet und führte zu einer Woge experimenteller
Entwürfe, von stapelbaren Containern bis zur perfek-
tionierten Entwicklung von Fertigteilsystemen. Aus
dieser Linie des »High-Tech-Stils« gingen zwei bedeutende Architekten hervor, die die Ideen von Archigram Jahre später in der Praxis verwirklichten, Richard
Rogers und Norman Foster.
Nach anfänglicher Zusammenarbeit mit Foster eröff-
nete Rogers sein eigenes Büro und verfolgte eine
mehr plastisch-expressive Linie der High-Tech-Archi-
tektur. In Zusammenarbeit mit Renzo Piano realisierte
Rogers die Formensprache des Archigram-Projektes
»Plug-in City« (1964–1966) gekonnt beim Centre
Pompidou in Paris (1971–1977) und noch einmal beim
Lloyd's Verwaltungsgebäude in London (1982).
Norman Fosters Arbeiten erinnern an Projekte des
Engländers Cedric Price, eines weiteren englischen
Vertreters der »arthropodischen« Architektur. Price
stellte sich für seinen Fun Palace (1961–1964) eine
industrielle Megastruktur mit Haut vor. Ebendiese
Idee lag auch Fosters Versicherungsgebäude Willis
Faber & Dumas zugrunde, das er 1975 in Ipswich
baute. In einer Zeit, in der eine entschiedene Architek-
turgestaltung fast verpönt war, entwickelte Foster mit
diesem Gebäude eine Ästhetik der Gegenstandslosigkeit: ein Rückgriff auf Mittel der klassischen Moderne. Die totale Verglasung eines gekurvten Gebäudes bot eine neue Möglichkeit der Abstraktion und
gleichzeitig einen genialen Ausweg aus der aggressi-
ven Körperlichkeit des Funktionalismus der siebziger
Jahre. Die Wiederentdeckung des konsequent glä-

de collages linéaires graphiquement nouveaux et
abstraits enthousiasme une armée d'épigones. Berlin
constitue un pôle de repos positif dans les recherches
adaptées et tactiques des courants compétitifs allemands. Pour finir, le manque de conscience de soi de
l'architecture allemande se reflète dans la peur du
principe de l'esthétique. Les revues allemandes d'architecture ressemblent davantage à des bulletins ju-
ridiques qu'aux excellentes publications créatrices
existant par exemple en Italie ou en Espagne.

ANGLETERRE

Au milieu des années 60, par suite du Pop Art, une
architecture de refus »arthropodique« utopique qui
peut être considérée comme précurseur de la déconstruction, a vu le jour. Quelques années plus tard,
on comptait parmi les principaux représentants le
groupe autrichien Haus-Rucker-Co (dissout en 1991)
qui travaillent à Düsseldorf, Coop Himmelblau et le
groupe londonien Archigram avec son protagoniste
Peter Cook. C'est avant tout le groupe Archigram qui
a lancé des impulsions décisives dans l'architecture
européenne. Le message critique d'un monde fictif
superfuturiste fut interprété affirmativement – dans
l'euphorie technologique des années 70 – par de
nombreux architectes et aboutit à une vague de projets expérimentaux allant des conteneurs empilables
au développement perfectionné de systèmes d'éléments unifiés. Richard Rogers et Norman Foster, deux
éminents architectes anglais qui ont réalisé dans la
pratique les idées d'Archigram quelques années plus
tard, sont sortis de cette ligne du style »high tech«.
Après avoir collaboré avec Foster au début, Rogers
ouvrit son propre bureau et suivit une ligne plus plastique et plus expressive de l'architecture high tech. En
collaboration avec Renzo Piano, Rogers a réalisé
avec beaucoup de savoir-faire le langage formel du
programme d'Archigram »Plug-in City« (1964–1966)
au Centre Pompidou à Paris (1972–1977) et une fois
encore dans le bâtiment administratif Lloyd's à Londres (1982).
Les constructions de Norman Foster rappellent les
projets de Cedric Price, autre représentant anglais de
l'architecture »arthropodique«. Pour son Fun Palace
(1961/64), Price a imaginé une mégastructure industrielle avec une membrane. C'est justement cette idée
qui était également à la base du bâtiment d'assu-
rance Willis Faber & Dumas que Foster construisit en
1975 à Ipswich. A une époque où un conception
architecturale résolue était presque vue d'une mau-
vais œil, Foster développa avec ce bâtiment un esthétique de la non-figuration: un recours à des moyens
du modernisme classique. Le vitrage complet d'un
édifice aux formes courbes offrait une nouvelle possi-

Richard Rogers Partnership, Lloyd's
Building in London, Great Britain,
1979–1986 (opposite page)

Nicholas Grimshaw & Partners, Financial Times Printing Works, London,
Great Britain, 1987–1988

James Stirling, Michael Wilford, Tate
Gallery in Liverpool, Great Britain, 1988
(above and opposite page)

framework, make Foster one of the leading purveyors of revitalized European Modernism. He has also exerted a clear influence upon the German competition scene, which has adopted his abstractive drawing technique.

James Stirling is an exception amongst European architects. He has worked in partnership with Michael Wilford for many years. His strong sense of historical lines of development led him to produce expressive buildings with a powerful feeling for form in as early as the fifties. The most important works of this period include Leicester University Engineering Building (1959–1963) and the Cambridge University History Faculty Building (1964–1967). Both of these bold designs were effectively a rediscovery of Russian Constructivism, a fact his contemporaries failed to observe. Even Stirling's earliest designs betrayed his unusual interest in the themes of urban space and history – themes which became particularly contemporary in the seventies, when a number of international competitions were held for the design of new museum buildings during the economic boom in West Germany. In his competition designs for Düsseldorf (1975), Cologne (1976) and Stuttgart (1980), Stirling developed an architectural language of monumentality and historicity – unmistakable elements of Post-Modernism. Together with his pupils Rob and Leon Krier, he lifted post-war Germany's taboos on the aesthetics of monumentality and urban space. It was his response to this latter theme that won him the competition for the state art gallery in Stuttgart. Stirling exploits destroyed urban landscapes as rich settings for his expressive compositions. In the wake of Post-Modernism, his design style has changed from one of expressive modernity in the spirit of the Russian avantgarde to one of historical collage, and stamped by a subtle symbolism. Unlike others such as Michael Graves and Charles Moore, Stirling has never used history simply as decoration, however, but as a field of research which he explores with his designs. His borrowings from history are always subordinate to his overall design strategy, namely urban repair using a remedial form deduced from the damaged environment (contextualism). His more recent works offer new thoughts on figural composition. His philosophical bent is giving way to a new Expressionism.

Experienced »master architects« such as Rogers, Foster and Stirling dominate the English architectural scene. The sensational avant-garde performance and stimulating innovations of the sixties and seventies have ceased. Instead, in Richmond, Quinlan Terry is building in the most perfected strain of historicism in Europe! The majority of young English designers work at a modest regional level. Surprises have appeared

sernen Curtainwalls im Sinne von Mies van der Rohes Glashochhaus (1921) und die konsequente Entwicklung einer neuen Ästhetik des Tragwerks machen Foster zu einem der führenden Vertreter der erneuerten europäischen Moderne. Ihm ist auch ein deutlicher Einfluß auf die deutsche Wettbewerbsszene zuzusprechen, die seine abstrahierende Zeichentechnik übernommen hat.

James Stirling ist eine Ausnahmeerscheinung unter den europäischen Architekten. Seit Jahren arbeitet er mit Michael Wilford zusammen. Durch seinen ausgeprägten Sinn für historische Entwicklungslinien gelang es ihm schon in den fünfziger Jahren, mit expressivem Formgefühl ausdrucksvolle Gebäude zu entwerfen. Die bedeutendsten Bauten dieser Zeit sind ein Universitätsgebäude in Leicester (1959–1963) und ein Universitätsgebäude in Cambridge (1964–1967). Eigentlich handelt es sich bei diesen kühnen Entwürfen um eine Wiederentdeckung des russischen Konstruktivismus, was seine Zeitgenossen nicht bemerkten. Schon in seinen ersten Entwürfen zeigte Stirling ein außerordentliches Interesse an den Themen Stadtraum und Geschichte – Themen, die in den siebziger Jahren an Aktualität gewannen, als im westdeutschen Konjunkturboom internationale Wettbewerbe für Museen ausgeschrieben wurden. Bei den Museumswettbewerben in Düsseldorf 1975, Köln 1976 und Stuttgart 1980 entwickelte Stirling eine Architektursprache der Monumentalität und Geschichtlichkeit: unverkennbare Elemente der Postmoderne. Gemeinsam mit seinen Schülern Rob und Leon Krier enttabuisierte er im Nachkriegsdeutschland die Ästhetik der Monumen-

bilité d'abstraction et en même temps une issue géniale à la matérialité agressive du fonctionnalisme des années 70. La redécouverte du mur-rideau conséquemment en verre au sens du gratte-ciel en verre de Mies van der Rohe (1921) et le développement logique d'une nouvelle esthétique de la structure porteuse font de Foster l'un des représentants les plus éminents du style moderne européen renouvelé. On doit également lui attribuer une nette influence sur la scène compétitive allemande qui a repris sa technique graphique abstractive.

James Stirling est un phénomène exceptionnel parmi les architectes européens. Depuis des années, il travaille avec Michael Wilford. Grâce à un sens prononcé pour les lignes de développement historiques, il est parvenu dès les années 50 à projeter des bâtiments éloquents avec un sens formel expressif. Les édifices les plus remarquables de cette époque sont un bâtiment universitaire à Leicester (1959–1963) et un bâtiment universitaire à Cambridge (1964–1967). A vrai dire, il s'agit dans ces projets audacieux d'une redécouverte du constructivisme russe, ce que ses contemporains n'ont pas remarqué. Dans ses premiers projets, Stirling avait déjà montré un intérêt extraordinaire pour les thèmes espace urbain et histoire, thèmes qui devinrent actuels dans les années 70 lorsque des consultations internationales pour des musées furent ouvertes par suite de l'essor conjoncturel ouest-allemand. Pour les concours des musées de Düsseldorf (1975), Cologne (1976) et Stuttgart (1980), Stirling a développé un langage architectural de la monumentalité et du savoir-faire: éléments évidents du postmodernisme. Avec ses élèves Rob et Leon Krier, il a détabouisé l'esthétique de la monumentalité et de l'espace urbain dans l'Allemagne de l'après-guerre. Avec ce dernier thème, il est parvenu à gagner le concours pour la Staatsgalerie de Stuttgart et à réaliser la construction. Stirling découvre les paysages urbains détruits comme un riche champ d'activité pour ses compositions urbaines expressives. Par suite du postmodernisme, son style d'étude est passé du modernisme expressionniste dans l'esprit de l'avant-garde russe à une technique de collage d'architecture historique. Elle est déterminée par un subtil symbolisme. Stirling n'a à vrai dire jamais employé l'histoire de l'architecture pour décorer, comme l'on fait par exemple Michael Graves ou Charles Moore, mais en tant que champ de recherches qu'il explore stratégiquement avec ses projets. Les décors mobiles de l'histoire se soumettent toujours à sa stratégie d'étude essentielle: réparer l'espace urbain détruit avec une forme contraire dérivée (contextualisme). Dans ses récents travaux, il montre de nouvelles possibilités de compositions fi-

only in the field of industrial architecture, as in works by Ian Ritchie (office building in Stockley Park) and Nicholas Grimshaw (Financial Times Printing Works). Stimulus amongst the younger generation is being provided by immigrant architects from other European nations. These include Leon Krier from Luxembourg, who works in London and whom even Prince Charles has singled out as the secret hope for England's architectural salvation. Krier attempts to change the unavoidable. His obssesive excursions into the nineteenth century in drawings and models invoke the past, create alternative worlds to the market economy – that driving force of architecture – and have prompted widespread discussion over the past decade. Unlike his teacher Stirling, Krier makes a philosophy of the architectural façades and artist craftmanship of the nineteenth century.

THE NETHERLANDS

The general level of architecture in the Netherlands can be said unreservedly to be the highest in Europe. The Netherlands does not suffer from the polarisation, such as seen in Italy and Germany, between theory-laden, critical show-case architecture on the one hand and general architectural practice on the other.

Ian Ritchie, Office Building B8 in Stockley Park, Great Britain, 1988–1990

talität und des Stadtraums. Mit dem letztgenannten Thema gelang es ihm, den Wettbewerb für die Staatsgalerie in Stuttgart zu gewinnen und den Bau zu realisieren. Stirling entdeckt die zerstörten Stadtlandschaften als reiches Betätigungsfeld für seine expressiven stadträumlichen Kompositionen. Im Zuge der Postmoderne wandelte sich sein Entwurfsstil von der expressionistischen Moderne im Geist der russischen Avantgarde zu einer Collagetechnik historischer Architektur. Sie ist von einem feinsinnigen Symbolismus bestimmt. Stirling hat die Architekturgeschichte aber eigentlich nie zur Dekoration benutzt, wie etwa Michael Graves oder Charles Moore, sondern als Forschungsgebiet, das er strategisch mit seinen Entwürfen abtastet. Die Versatzstücke der Geschichte ordnen sich immer seiner wesentlichen Entwurfsstrategie unter: den zerstörten Stadtraum mit einer abgeleiteten Gegenform zu reparieren (Kontextualismus). In neueren Arbeiten zeigt er neue Möglichkeiten figürlicher Kompositionen, sein philosophisches Anliegen weicht einem neuen Expressionismus.

Erfahrene »Meisterarchitekten« wie Rogers, Foster und Stirling dominieren die englische Architekturszene. Aufsehenerregende Avantgardeleistungen und innovative Impulse wie in den sechziger und siebziger Jahren sind nicht mehr zu verzeichnen. Quinlan Terry baut statt dessen in Richmond den perfektesten Historismus in Europa! Die meisten jungen Entwerfer arbeiten auf bescheidenem regionalem Niveau. Lediglich die Industriearchitektur zeigt teilweise überraschende Ergebnisse, wie Arbeiten von Ian Ritchie (Bürogebäude im Stockley Park) und Nicholas Grimshaw (Druckerei Financial Times). Entscheidende Impulse aus der nachfolgenden Generation kommen von Einwanderern aus anderen europäischen Ländern. Dazu zählt der Luxemburger Leon Krier, der in London arbeitet und selbst von Prinz Charles als Geheimtip für die architektonische Rettung Englands entdeckt wurde. Krier versucht, das Unvermeidliche zu ändern. Seine obsessiven Rückgriffe auf das 19. Jahrhundert in Zeichnungen und Modellen beschwören die Vergangenheit, erzeugen Gegenwelten zum Architekturmotor Marktwirtschaft und haben im vergangenen Jahrzehnt breite Diskussionen ausgelöst. Anders als sein Lehrer Stirling macht Krier die Architekturfassaden und die Handwerkskunst des 19. Jahrhunderts zu einer Weltanschauung.

NIEDERLANDE

Man kann ohne Vorbehalte sagen, daß die niederländische Architekturpraxis in ihrem allgemeinen Niveau auf dem höchsten Stand in Europa ist. Eine Polarisierung zwischen einer theorielastigen, kritischen Galeriearchitektur auf der einen und der breiten Architek-

gurées. Sa préoccupation philosophique fait place à un nouvel expressionnisme.

Des »architectes experts« tels que Rogers, Foster et Stirling dominent la scène architecturale anglaise. On ne note plus de sensationnelles réalisations avant-gardistes et d'impulsions innovatrices comme dans les années 60 et 70. Au lieu de cela, Quinlan Terry construit à Richmond l'éclectisme le plus parfait en Europe! La plupart des jeunes concepteurs anglais travaillent à un modeste niveau régional. Seule l'architecture industrielle présente en partie de surprenants résultats comme les œuvres de Ian Ritchie (édifice dans Stockley Park) et Nicholas Grimshaw (Imprimerie Financial Times). Les impulsions décisives de la génération suivante proviennent d'immigrés issus d'autres pays européens. Le Luxembourgeois Leon Krier, qui travaille à Londres et que le prince Charles a qualifié de »tuyau« pour le salut architectonique de l'Angleterre, en fait partie. Krier tente de corriger l'inévitable. Les recours répétés au XIXe siècle, que l'on peut observer dans ses dessins et ses maquettes, évoquent le passé, créent des mondes opposés au moteur architectural qu'est l'économie de marché et ont déclenché de vastes discussions au cours de la décennie passée. A la différence de son professeur Stirling, Krier fait des façades architectoniques et de l'art artisanal du XIXe siècle une idéologie.

PAYS-BAS

On peut dire sans réserves que la pratique architecturale néerlandaise occupe généralement la position la plus élevée en Europe. Aux Pays-Bas, il n'y a pas de polarisation entre une architecture critique et théorétique pour les galeries d'une part et la pratique architecturale générale d'autre part, comme nous les connaissons en Italie et en Allemagne. Comment peut-on expliquer cela? Depuis le Moyen-Age finissant, les Pays-Bas ont été, en tant que pays de marins, l'une des régions marchandes les plus importantes et les plus riches. Ceci s'exprime dans l'étonnante abondance de volumes bâtis d'une grande valeur historique que l'on trouve particulièrement dans les régions côtières. La construction en clinker expressionniste de l'Ecole d'Amsterdam (1906–1920) qui, dans sa différenciation et sa spatialité, a établi des critères pour les habitations à bon marché dans toute l'Europe, est également basée sur cette tradition. Aux Pays-Bas, la pénurie de sols a toujours abouti à d'intéressantes expériences de la concentration architecturale. Dans les années 70, les structuralistes Herman Hertzberger, Aldo van Eyck et Frank van Klingeren ont acquis une grande influence. Leur interprétation sensible de la construction à base d'éléments unifiés est essentielle comparée aux constructions européennes de l'épo-

Why not? As a nation of seafarers, Holland has been one of the richest and most important trading regions since the late Middle Ages. This is reflected in its remarkable wealth of historical architecture, found in particular in coastal areas. The Expressionist brick architecture of the School of Amsterdam (1906–20) is based on this same tradition. Its differentiation and spaciousness has set standards for state-built housing across Europe. Structuralists Herman Hertzberger, Aldo van Eyck and Frank van Klingeren gained considerable influence in the seventies. Significant is their sensitive interpretation of prefabricated architecture compared to the rest of Europe at this time.

Dutch architecture today preserves an almost unbroken relationship with its own past. The cultivation of design in public spaces is also a striking feature of the Netherlands. It is no coincidence that the Netherlands produced its own Modern Movement in the De Stijl group. Alongside the Expressionism of the School of Amsterdam, the De Stijl aesthetic prompted a second line of development in Dutch architecture which is pursued even today in the polychrome works of the OMA group. OMA – the Office for Metropolitan Architecture – was founded in London in 1980 by Rem Koolhaas, Elia Zenghelis, and the painters Zoe Zenghelis and Madelon Vriesendorp. Koolhaas personifies the architectural genius of the new generation, exerting a profound influence on the European architectural scene. In 1975 he worked under Ungers on the competition design for the Wallraf-Richartz-Museum in Cologne. From Ungers he learned to link theory and practical design and the methodology of complex collage in urban planning. By the beginning of the eighties, his logical pursuit of this design methodology on the basis of the rediscovered Suprematist architecture of Russian Modernism had resulted in drawings and models which attracted international attention.

There are a large number of Dutch artists who design to very high standards but who have so far failed to gain international recognition. These include Jo Coenen, Sjoerd Soeters, Jan Benthem and Mels Crouwel. Many original and differentiated designs have been made since the eighties within the field of experimental industrial architecture in particular. Contemporary Dutch architecture overall reveals a clear trend towards a return to the style of classical Modernism.

FRANCE

Architecture in France has been a sorry scene of stylistic experiment right up to the eighties. It lacks the traditions left elsewhere by major schools of Expressionism and the influential Modern Movements of the

Ton Alberts, Max von Hunt, Headquarters of NMB Bank, Amsterdam, Netherlands, 1979–1987

turpraxis auf der anderen Seite, wie wir sie in Italien und Deutschland kennen, gibt es in den Niederlanden nicht. Wie ist dies zu erklären? Seit dem späten Mittelalter sind die Niederlande als Seefahrernation eine der bedeutendsten und reichsten Handelsregionen gewesen. Dies drückt sich in der erstaunlichen Fülle historisch wertvoller Bausubstanz aus, die wir besonders in den Küstenregionen antreffen. Auf dieser Tradition basiert auch die expressionistische Klinkerarchitektur der Amsterdamer Schule (1906–1920), die in ihrer Differenzierung und Räumlichkeit Maßstäbe für den sozialen Wohnungsbau in ganz Europa gesetzt hat. Die Bodenknappheit hat in den Niederlanden immer wieder zu interessanten Experimenten der Architekturverdichtung geführt. In den siebziger Jahren gewannen die Strukturalisten Herman Hertzberger, Aldo van Eyck und Frank van Klingeren großen Einfluß. Bedeutend ist ihre feinfühlige Interpretation der Fertigteilarchitektur im europäischen Vergleich dieser Zeit. Die aktuelle Architektur hat ein weitgehend ungebrochenes Verhältnis zur eigenen Geschichte. Außerdem findet man in den Niederlanden eine bemerkenswerte Kultivierung des Designs im öffentlichen Raum.

Es ist kein Zufall, daß die Niederlande mit der Gruppe De Stijl eine eigene Quelle der frühen Moderne hervorgebracht haben. Neben dem Expressionismus der Amsterdamer Schule ist es die De-Stijl-Ästhetik, von der eine zweite Entwicklungslinie der niederländischen Architektur ausgeht, die sich bis heute in den polychromen Arbeiten der Gruppe OMA fortsetzt. Das Office for Metropolitan Architecture wurde 1975 in London von Rem Koolhaas, Elia Zenghelis und den Malerinnen Zoe Zenghelis und Madelon Vriesendorp gegründet. Koolhaas verkörpert den genialen Architekten der neuen Generation, der die europäische Architekturszene richtungsweisend beeinflußt. Er arbeitete mit Peter Eisenman am Institute for Architecture and Urban Studies und mit Ungers, u. a. beim Wettbewerb für das Wallraf-Richartz-Museum in Köln, zusammen. Von Ungers lernte er die Verbindung von Theorie und praktischem Entwurf und die Methodik der komplexen Collage im Städtebau. Die konsequente Fortsetzung dieser Entwurfsmethodik auf der Basis der wiederentdeckten suprematischen Konstruktion der russischen Moderne führte schon Anfang der achtziger Jahre zu Zeichnungen und Modellen, die international Aufmerksamkeit erregten.

Es gibt eine große Zahl niederländischer Architekten, die auf sehr hohem Niveau entwerfen, aber international bislang wenig Beachtung gefunden haben. Dazu gehören Jo Coenen, Sjoerd Soeters, Jan Benthem und Mels Crouwel. Besonders im experimentellen Industriebau sind seit den achtziger Jahren viele

que. L'architecture actuelle a un rapport généralement farouche avec sa propre histoire. On trouve en outre aux Pays-Bas une culture remarquable du design dans les bâtiments publics.

Ce n'est pas un hasard si les Pays-Bas ont engendré une source propre du modernisme des débuts avec le groupe »De Stijl«. A côté de l'expressionnisme de l'Ecole d'Amsterdam, c'est l'esthétique du mouvement De Stijl, dont part une deuxième tendance de l'architecture néerlandaise, qui se poursuit jusqu'à ce jour dans les œuvres polychromes du groupe OMA. L'Office for Metropolitan Architectur a été fondé en 1975 à Londres par Rem Koolhaas, Elia Zenghelis et les peintres Zoe Zenghelis et Madelon Vriesendorp. Koolhaas incarne l'architecte génial de la nouvelle génération, qui influence de façon déterminante la scène architecturale européenne. Il a travaillé avec Peter Eisenman à l'Institute for Architecture and Urban Studios et avec Ungers, entre autres à l'occasion du concours pour le musée Wallraf-Richartz à Cologne. Ungers lui a appris à allier la théorie et le projet pratique, de même que la méthodique du collage complexe en urbanisme. La suite logique de cette méthodique d'étude sur la base de la construction dominante redécouverte du modernisme russe a déjà produit des dessins et des maquettes qui ont attiré l'attention internationale au début des années 80.

Bon nombre d'architectes néerlandais font des projets de haut niveau, mais ont jusqu'ici trouvé peu de considération au niveau international. Jo Coenen, Sjoerd Soeters, Jan Benthem et Mels Crouwel en font partie. C'est surtout dans la construction industrielle expérimentale que beaucoup de projets différenciés et riches en idées ont vu le jour depuis 1980. Dans l'ensemble, l'architecture néerlandaise actuelle montre aussi de nettes tendances au renouement avec le style du modernisme classique.

FRANCE

Jusque dans les années 80, la scène architecturale française a montré une lamentable image d'expérience stylistique. Il manque la tradition d'une grande école expressionniste ou d'une influente école du mouvement moderne dans les années 20. Le Corbusier, architecte d'origine suisse et le plus important architecte européen de cette époque, a construit en France jusque dans les années 60, mais est toujours resté un étranger pour les Français.

Henri Ciriani, l'un des influents maîtres du modernisme, reprend des éléments stylistiques de l'œuvre des débuts du Corbusier, mais il ne parvient pas à l'interprétation géniale d'un Richard Meier. On remarquera que la construction française qui a le plus attiré l'attention dans les années 70, le Centre Pompi-

Architecture Studio, Lycée du Future in Poitiers, France, 1987 (above)

Johan Otto von Spreckelsen, Paul Andreu, L'Arche de la Défense in Paris, France, 1984–1989 (opposite page)

twenties. Although Le Corbusier – Swiss by birth and the most important European architect of the age – continued building in France until the sixties, to the French he has always remained a foreigner.

While Henri Ciriani, one of the Modern Movement's influential teachers, adapted stylistic elements from Le Corbusier's early work, he failed to equal the sympathetic interpetation of such as Richard Meier. It is noteworthy that the most respected French building of the seventies, the Centre Pompidou, was an English-Italian co-production (1977, Richard Rogers with Renzo Piano). Similarly, the most spectacular design of the late eighties, the La Defense conglomerate, sprang not from a French mind but from the Danish architect Johan Otto von Spreckelsen. But once the initial impact of the sheer size of La Defense has passed, the visitor is left with a more lasting impression of an architecture designed for a world without people. The post-modern projects around Paris by the Spaniard Ricardo Bofill reflect this same French preference for architectural gigantism beyond human

ideenreiche und differenzierte Entwürfe entstanden. Insgesamt zeigt auch die aktuelle niederländische Architektur deutliche Tendenzen zur Wiederanknüpfung an den Stil der klassischen Moderne.

FRANKREICH

Die Architekturszene in Frankreich vermittelte bis in die achtziger Jahre hinein ein klägliches Bild stilistischer Experimente. Es fehlt die Tradition einer bedeutenden expressionistischen Schule oder einer einflußreichen Schule der Moderne in den zwanziger Jahren. Le Corbusier, der gebürtige Schweizer und bedeutendste europäische Architekt dieser Zeit, hat zwar noch bis in die sechziger Jahre in Frankreich gebaut, ist aber den Franzosen immer ein Fremder geblieben. Henri Ciriani, einer der einflußreichen Lehrer der Moderne, nimmt zwar stilistische Elemente des frühen Werks Le Corbusiers auf, erreicht dabei aber nicht die kongeniale Interpretation eines Richard Meier. Es ist bemerkenswert, daß das am meisten beachtete französische Bauwerk der siebziger Jahre, das Centre

dou, était une coproduction anglo-italienne et que le projet le plus spectaculaire de la fin des années 80, la Tête Défense, conçu par l'architecte danois Johan Otto von Spreckelsen, n'est pas non plus d'origine française. Le conglomérat de la Défense impressionne le visiteur de passage par sa grandeur: mais ensuite, on a l'impression d'avoir affaire à une architecture pour un monde sans êtres humains. Les projets postmodernes réalisés par l'Espagnol Ricardo Bofill autour de Paris expriment également le penchant des Français pour un gigantisme architectural démesuré. Le fait que Paris se soit transformé par endroits en un monstrueux chaos est peut-être dû à une crise d'identité culturelle, à une fausse ambition et à une indécision entre la tradition et le progrès.

Christian de Portzamparc et ses projets de construction de logements aux formes expressives ont été remarqués dans la phase du postmodernisme. Portzamparc a fait ses études à l'Ecole Nationale Supérieure des Beaux-Arts. Avant de s'établir, il a travaillé dans les ateliers d'Eugène Beaudouin et de Georges

Renzo Piano Building Workshop, Extension of the Institute for Acoustics/Music Research and Coordination in Paris, France, 1988–1989 (opposite page)

Jean Nouvel, Architecture Studio,
Interior of the Institut du Monde Arabe
in Paris, France, 1984–1987

Bernard Tschumi, Folies in the Parc de
la Villette in Paris, France, 1982–1991

scale. The monstrous chaos that Paris has in places become may perhaps be explained in terms of a cultural identity crisis, false pride and an inability to choose between tradition and progress.

In the era of Post-Modernism, Christian de Portzamparc gained a reputation with his expressively modelled housing projects. Portzamparc studied at the Ecole Nationale Supérieur des Beaux-Arts. He worked under Eugène Beaudouin and Georges Candilis before setting up alone. His most recent projects are neo-Modernist urban ensembles in the polychrome style of the OMA group.

The Paris exhibition of young French architects in spring 1991 included a series of designs taking up international trends ranging from Arata Isozaki to Rem Koolhaas. Younger French architects pursuing a colourful interpretation of classical Modernism include Jean François Schmit, Françoise Fromonot & Antoine Belin, the Arca 2 group and Joseph Almudever with Christian Lefèvre. Amongst the established architectural practices, Jean Pierre Buffi & Associés are designing in the style of precise, monumental Futurism. Their current project, »Les Collines«, is a development around the Grande Arche in Paris-La-Défense.

The figure of Jean Nouvel stands out from the body of French architects at the start of the nineties. He takes the science fiction films of Ridley Scott and Peter Hyams as a major source of his inspiration. Nouvel gained international recognition with his Arabian Cultural Institute (1987) in Paris. With a devastating logic, his recent designs develop abstract-cubist forms and thereby force modernism towards a monumental Futurism. His tendency towards the principles of reduction, perfection and repetition recall the young Mies van der Rohe. Nouvel designs huge glass cuboids with screen façades; architectonic embodiments of the new age of the computer and total information.

Bernard Tschumi, born in Switzerland and now with offices in Paris and New York, is one of the leading representatives of French deconstructivism. In his structures for the Parc de la Villette (1982–1991) he seeks to revitalize the formal principles of the Russian avant-garde from Konstantin Melnikov to El Lissitzky. In his design studies he is like a comic-strip artist, working freely along the lines of Suprematist architecture. His works are reinforced by theory and the new concept of »architectural disjunction«.

ITALY

Contemporary Italian architecture is part of a tradition going as far back as Leon Battista Alberti and Andrea Palladio, in which the marriage of theory and practice

Pompidou, eine englisch-italienische Koproduktion war und der spektakulärste Entwurf Ende der achtziger Jahre, die Arche de la Defense des dänischen Architekten Johan Otto von Spreckelsen, ebenfalls nicht französischen Ursprungs ist. Das ganze Konglomerat La Defense beeindruckt den Kurzbesucher ob seiner schieren Größe; dann jedoch setzt sich der Eindruck durch, man habe es hier mit einer Architektur für eine Welt ohne Menschen zu tun. Auch die postmodernen Projekte des Spaniers Ricardo Bofill um Paris drücken die Neigung der Franzosen zu einem maßstabslosen Architekturgigantismus aus. Vielleicht ist es einer kulturellen Identitätskrise, falschem Ehrgeiz und Unentschlossenheit zwischen Tradition und Fortschritt zuzuschreiben, daß sich Paris stellenweise in ein monströses Chaos verwandelt hat.

In der Phase der Postmoderne fiel Christian de Portzamparc mit expressiv geformten Wohnungsbauprojekten auf. Portzamparc studierte an der Ecole Nationale Supérieure des Beaux-Arts. Vor seiner Selbständigkeit arbeitete er in den Ateliers von Eugène Beaudouin und Georges Candilis. Bei Projekten aus jüngster Zeit zeigt er neomoderne Stadtensembles im polychromen Stil der Gruppe OMA.

Auf der Pariser Ausstellung junger französischer Architekten im Frühjahr 1991 war eine Reihe von Entwürfen zu sehen, die internationale Strömungen von Arata Isozaki bis Rem Koolhaas aufnehmen. Von den jüngeren französischen Architekten, die meist eine farbige Interpretation der klassischen Moderne verfolgen, sind u. a. zu nennen: Jean François Schmit, Françoise Fromonot & Antoine Belin, die Gruppe Arca 2 und Joseph Almudever mit Christian Lefèvre. Von den etablierten Büros entwirft in der Linie des monumentalen, präzisen Futurismus Jean Pierre Buffi & Associés. Ihr aktuelles Projekt ist eine Bebauung um die Grande Arche, »Les Collines«, in Paris-La-Défense.

Die herausragende Gestalt unter den französischen Architekten ist Anfang der neunziger Jahre Jean Nouvel. Eine entscheidende Inspirationsquelle für seine Arbeiten sind die Science-fiction-Filme von Ridley Scott und Peter Hyams. International bekannt wurde Nouvel mit dem arabischen Kulturinstitut in Paris (1987). Mit einer verblüffenden Konsequenz entwirft er in neueren Arbeiten abstrakt-kubische Figuren und treibt dabei die Moderne in Richtung eines monumentalen Futurismus. Seine Neigung zu den Prinzipien Reduktion, Perfektion und Wiederholung erinnern an den jungen Mies van der Rohe. Nouvel entwirft gewaltige gläserne Quader mit Bildschirmfassaden: architektonische Verkörperungen des neuen Zeitalters der Computer und der totalen Information.

Der gebürtige Schweizer Bernard Tschumi mit Büros in

Candilis. Dans ses projets récents, il montre des ensembles urbains néo-modernes dans le style polychrome du groupe OMA.

Au printemps 1991, on a pu voir à l'exposition parisienne des jeunes architectes français des projets qui reprennent des tendances internationales allant de Arata Isozaki à Rem Koolhaas. Parmi les jeunes architectes français, qui suivent généralement une interprétation colorée du modernisme classique, nous citerons entre autres: Jean François Schmit, Françoise Fromonot & Antoine Belin, le groupe Arca 2 et Joseph Almudever avec Christian Lefèvre. Parmi les bureaux établis, Jean Pierre Buffi & Associés projettent dans la ligne du futurisme monumental et précis. Leur projet actuel est un aménagement urbain autour de la Grande Arche, »Les Collines«, à Paris-La-Défense.

Jean Nouvel est la personnalité marquante parmi les architectes français du début des années 90. Les films de science-fiction de Ridley Scott et de Peter Hyams constituent une source d'inspiration essentielle pour ses projets. Nouvel a obtenu la célébrité internationale avec l'Institut culturel du monde arabe à Paris en 1987. Avec une logique stupéfiante, il dessine dans ses récents projets des figures cubiques abstraites, poussant ainsi le modernisme vers un futurisme monumental. Sa tendance aux principes réduction, perfection et répétition rappelle le jeune Mies van der Rohe. Nouvel conçoit d'imposants parallélipipèdes en verre avec des façades-écrans: incarnations architectoniques de la nouvelle ère de l'ordinateur et de l'information totale.

Bernard Tschumi, qui est né en Suisse et a des bureaux à New York et à Paris, est considéré comme important représentant du déconstructivisme français. Avec les édifices du Parc de La Villette (1982–1991), il entreprend de revitaliser les principes formels de l'avant-garde russe de Konstantin Melnikov jusqu'à El Lissitzky. Ses études rappellent les auteurs de bandes dessinées qui dessinent au hasard, insouciants, sur les traces de la construction suprématique. Il complète ses œuvres spatiales dynamiques par une théorie et la nouvelle notion de »disjonction architecturale«.

ITALIE

L'architecture italienne actuelle renoue avec une tradition dans laquelle la connexion de la théorie et de la pratique a joué un grand rôle depuis Leon Battista Alberti et Andrea Palladio. Les résultats de la pratique architecturale sont à peu près comparables à ceux de l'Allemagne. Ici et là, il existe un écart prononcé entre l'architecture urbaine et l'architecture rurale. Mais en Italie, la scène architecturale intellectualisée est plus

Aldo Rossi, social housing block in Berlin, Germany, 1989 (above)

Ignazio Gardella, New Faculty for Architecture in Genoa, Italy, 1990 (opposite page)

plays a major role. The products of Italian architectural practice are effectively comparable to those of Germany. Both countries reveal a pronounced difference in standard between town and country architecture. The intellectualized architectural scene in Italy is nevertheless more differentiated and sophisticated in spectrum, despite its narrower sphere of influence. The achievements of the Italian Renaissance play a central role in maintaining the high level of Italian architecture. They are present throughout Italy as a visible reality and continue to set standards for practising architects. In view of this tradition it is no coincidence that Italy was spared a ponderous traditionalism in the thirties, nor that classical Modernism has developed in Italy into a sensitive Rationalism with urbanistic aims. Alberto Libera and Giuseppe Terragni were important champions of this trend. Nor was Italy uprooted from its traditions after the war. Against this background, therefore, it is understandably difficult to assign the Italian architecture of the last two decades to the categories – modern or post-

New York und Paris gilt als ein bedeutender Vertreter des französischen Dekonstruktivismus. Mit den Bauten im Parc de La Villette (1982–1991) unternimmt er den Versuch, die Formprinzipien der russischen Avantgarde von Konstantin Melnikow bis El Lissitzky zu revitalisieren. Seine Entwurfsstudien erinnern an einen Comic-strip-Zeichner, der völlig unbekümmert auf den Spuren der suprematischen Konstruktion drauflosentwirft. Seine – weltraumdynamischen – Arbeiten ergänzt er mit einer Theorie und dem neuen Begriff der »Architekturdisjunktion«.

ITALIEN

Die aktuelle italienische Architektur knüpft an eine Tradition an, in der die Verbindung von Theorie und Praxis seit Leon Battista Alberti und Andrea Palladio eine große Rolle gespielt hat. Die Ergebnisse der Architekturpraxis sind in etwa denen in Deutschland vergleichbar. Hier wie dort gibt es ein ausgeprägtes Stadt-Land-Gefälle des Architekturniveaus. Aber das Spektrum der intellektualisierten Architekturszene in

différenciée et plus exigeante, bien que sa portée soit plus faible. Les grandes réalisations de la Renaissance italienne jouent un grand rôle pour le haut niveau de l'architecture italienne. Elles sont présentes dans toute l'Italie en tant que réalité architecturale et ont toujours établi des critères pour les architectes en exercice. Face à cette tradition, ce n'est pas un hasard si l'Italie a été épargnée par un traditionalisme grossier dans les années 30 et si le modernisme classique s'y est développé pour devenir un rationalisme subtil aux buts urbanistiques. Alberto Libera et Giuseppe Terragni ont été d'éminents représentants de cette tendance. Après la guerre, l'Italie n'a pas été déracinée du point de vue traditions. On peut donc comprendre que l'architecture italienne des deux dernières décennies ne pouvait guère être classée dans les catégories schématiques – moderne ou postmoderne – du critique d'architecture anglais Charles Jencks. L'architecture italienne de l'après-guerre a pu conjuguer l'art de l'ingénieur et la magie. L'architecte-ingénieur Pier Luigi Nervi (1891–1971), qui atteignit le

Aldo Rossi, Theatre of the World in
Venice, Italy, 1979

modern – identified by English architecture critic
Charles Jencks. Italian post-war architecture embraces both engineering and magic. Alongside Carlo
Scarpa (1906–1978), master of the metaphysical detail, the influence of engineer-architect Pier Luigi Nervi
(1891–1971), who reached the height of his career in
the early sixties, must be equally acknowledged.

Vittorio Gregotti, who taught in Palermo as from 1964
and later in Venice, embodies the ideal Italian architect, combining theory and practice in one large
office. He has mastered everything from regional
analysis and urban planning to the realization of pow-
erfully expressive architecture in the best Rationalist
tradition. Within the framework of the 1984 Berlin IBA,
his project for a residential building on the Lützow-
strasse displayed a supremely logical use of materials
and detail. Gregotti's design for the University of
Calabria shows the spacious ensemble of an ideal
town.

In his project for »Berlin morgen« (1991) he proposes
realistic solutions for carefully-staged urban renewal.
His configurations are not merely theoretical, but rep-
resent a practical development of the Rationalist urban designs of the thirties. His overlaying of historical
city contours with tightly-organized inner districts,
composed of intersections, avenues and squares, es-
tablishes an important basis for future European urban planning. This neo-Rationalism, represented in
Germany by Ungers, is still the best answer to the
chaos of our cities, and offers – aesthetically and
economically – the most effective and humane solution to urban concentration within the spectrum of
contemporary modernism.

Alongside Ungers, Aldo Rossi is acknowledged
worldwide as the key figure in the rediscovery of Rationalism. In 1966 – in a phase of theoretical activity –
he published »The Architecture of the City«, an important book, in a period in which architects were suffer-
ing a lack of direction. Through his works Rossi de-
plored the decline of aesthetic standards throughout
Europe as a whole. In the early seventies he completed a first block of flats in Milan. This was followed
by several school projects (Broni, Fagnano and Ulani)
and a cemetery in Modena. His activities in the eighties ranged from furniture design to urban planning
concepts. Rossi has designed projects in the USA,
Japan and throughout Europe. In 1988 he won the
competition for the German History Museum in Berlin.
At the core of Rossi's theoretical work lies the type, in
which design theory and practical relief strategy are
united. The formal patterns determined by such typical elements lean to a characteristic aesthetic. Thus
the harmonious cityscapes of previous eras can be
explained in terms of building type as design principle.

Italien ist trotz geringer Breitenwirkung differenzierter und anspruchsvoller. Für das hohe Niveau der italienischen Architektur spielen die bedeutenden Leistungen der italienischen Renaissance eine große Rolle. Sie sind in ganz Italien als bauliche Realität präsent und haben immer wieder Maßstäbe für praktizierende Architekten gesetzt. Mit Blick auf diese Tradition ist es kein Zufall, daß Italien in den dreißiger Jahren von einem plumpen Traditionalismus verschont geblieben ist und sich die klassische Moderne dort zu einem feinsinnigen Rationalismus mit städtebaulichen Zielen entwickelt hat. Bedeutende Vertreter dieser Richtung waren Alberto Libera und Giuseppe Terragni. Auch nach dem Krieg ist Italien nicht in seinen Traditionen entwurzelt worden. Vor diesem Hintergrund ist es zu verstehen, daß die italienische Architektur der letzten zwei Jahrzehnte kaum in die schematischen Kategorien – modern oder postmodern – des englischen Architekturkritikers Charles Jencks einzuordnen war. Die italienische Nachkriegsarchitektur vermochte Ingenieurkunst und Magie in sich zu vereinen. Der Ingenieurarchitekt Pier Luigi Nervi (1891–1971), der Anfang der sechziger Jahre den Höhepunkt seines Schaffens erreichte, muß als einflußreiche Architektengestalt ebenso genannt werden wie Carlo Scarpa (1906–1978), der Meister des metaphysischen Details.

Vittorio Gregotti, der seit 1964 zunächst in Palermo, danach in Venedig lehrt, verkörpert den Idealtyp des italienischen Architekten, der Theorie und Praxis in einem großen Büro zusammenführt. Er beherrscht das gesamte Spektrum von der regionalen Analyse über den stadträumlichen Entwurf bis hin zur Realisierung ausdrucksstarker Architektur in guter rationalistischer Tradition. 1984 fiel im Rahmen der IBA Berlin an der Lützowstraße ein Wohnungsbauprojekt auf, das durch eine verblüffend konsequente Verwendung von Material und Detail überraschte. Gregottis Entwurf für die Universität in Calabrien zeigt das weiträumige Ensemble einer Idealstadt.

Bei seinem Projekt für »Berlin morgen« (1991) demonstriert er realistische Möglichkeiten einer gut inszenierten Stadtreparatur. Seine stadträumlichen Figuren bleiben keine Theorie, sondern sind eine praktische Fortentwicklung der rationalistischen Stadtbaukunst der dreißiger Jahre. Die Überlagerung historischer Stadtgrundrisse mit spannungsvoll geordneten Quartieren, einem Ensemble von Achsen, Alleen und Plätzen, sind auch für die Zukunft des europäischen Städtebaus entscheidende Grundlagen. Dieser Neorationalismus, der in Deutschland von Ungers konsequent vertreten wird, ist immer noch die beste Antwort auf das Chaos der Städte; er bietet die – ästhetisch wie ökonomisch – wirkungsvollste und humanste Mög-

point culminant de sa carrière au début des années 60, doit être cité comme architecte influent, au même titre que Carlo Scarpa (1906–1978), le maître du détail métaphysique.

Vittorio Gregotti, qui enseigne depuis 1964, d'abord à Palerme, puis à Venise, incarne le type idéal de l'architecte italien réunissant la théorie et la pratique dans un grand bureau. Il domine tout l'éventail, depuis l'analyse régionale jusqu'à la réalisation d'une architecture expressive dans la bonne tradition rationaliste, en passant par le projet urbanistique. En 1984, un projet de construction de logements dans la Lützowstraße fut remarqué dans le cadre de l'IBA à Berlin, projet qui surprit par un emploi étonnamment logique des matériaux et des détails. Le projet conçu par Gregotti pour l'université de Calabre montre le vaste ensemble d'une ville idéale. Dans son projet pour »Berlin demain« (1991), il démontre des possibilités réalistes de réparation urbaine bien orchestrée. Ses figures urbanistiques ne restent pas théorie, mais sont un développement pratique de l'architecture urbaine rationaliste des années 30. La superposition de plans urbains historiques aux quartiers aménagés de manière captivante, un ensemble d'axes, d'allées et de places, sont aussi des bases décisives pour l'avenir de l'urbanisme européen. Ce néo-rationalisme, qui est représenté d'une manière conséquente par Ungers en Allemagne, est toujours la meilleure réponse au chaos des villes, il offre la possibilité la plus efficace et la plus humaine – esthétiquement et économiquement – de concentration urbaine dans la diversité du modernisme.

Aldo Rossi est considéré, outre O. M. Ungers, comme le personnage-clé du rationalisme redécouvert dans le monde entier. En 1966 – au cours d'une phase théorique – il a écrit son livre »L'architecture de la ville«, une œuvre capitale à une époque où les architectes étaient désorientés. Avec ses œuvres, Rossi a dénoncé la chute des valeurs esthétiques dans toute l'Europe. Au début des années 70, il a réalisé à Milan un premier immeuble d'habitation, qui fut suivi de quelques projets scolaires (Broni, Fagnano et Ulani) et d'un cimetière à Modène. Au début des années 80, ses projets allaient du design de meubles aux conceptions urbanistiques. Rossi conçoit des projets aux Etats-Unis, au Japon et en Europe. En 1988, il remporte le concours pour le Musée historique allemand à Berlin. Le noyau des travaux théoriques de Rossi est le type, qui réunit la théorie et la pratique comme stratégie décongestive. Les modèles formels déterminés par le type aboutissent à une esthétique caractéristique. Ainsi s'explique peut-être les harmonieux paysages urbains des époques passées à partir du type de construction en tant que principe d'étude. Les

Rossi concentrates his interest upon the type as focal construction task in the city (Theatre of the World, 1979), and upon industrially-manufactured objects. Rossi's formal vocabulary is governed by symmetrical references – on the pattern of geometrical ideal cities – and the purist formal constituents of the Italian Rationalism of the thirties. His dogged devotion to the essential elements of architecture results in forms and models which caution urgently against any final loss of the type.

Three names may be singled out by way of example from amongst the younger generation of Italian architects: Franco Stella, Francesco Venezia and Giorgio Grassi. In an office building in Thiene, Vincenza, in 1975, the Venetian Stella overlapped three different spatial situations to create a successful composition. Venezia's sculptural architecture – like that of Bienefeld in Germany – employs melancholic and mysterious symbols in the spirit of Carlo Scarpa. The Milanese Giorgio Grassi relentlessly pursues Rossi's call for architectural reduction to a monumental brick purism.

SWITZERLAND

Its geographical position and its multi-racial composition make Switzerland the most European of countries and at the same time a land of cultural division. The German-speaking North continues a Modernist trad-

Giorgio Grassi, entry for the
»Berlin morgen« exhibition, 1991

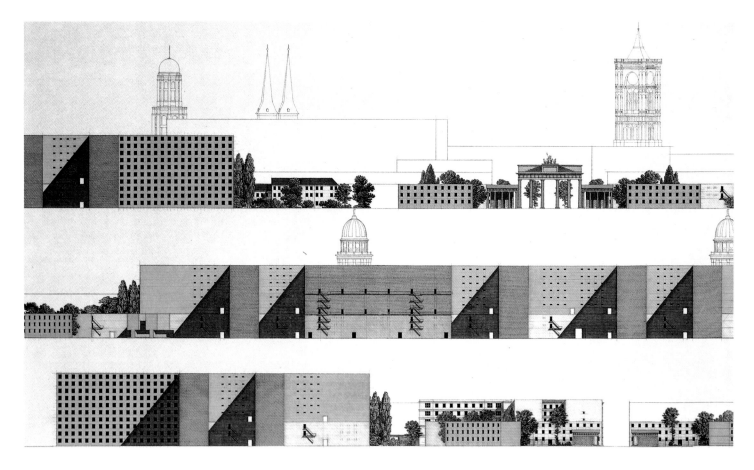

lichkeit der städtebaulichen Verdichtung im Spektrum der Moderne.

Aldo Rossi wird neben Ungers weltweit als die Schlüsselfigur des wiederentdeckten Rationalismus anerkannt. 1966 – in einer Phase theoretischer Arbeiten – entstand sein Buch »Die Architektur der Stadt«: ein bedeutendes Werk in einer Zeit großer Orientierungslosigkeit der Architekten. Mit seinen Arbeiten prangerte Rossi den Verfall ästhetischer Wertmaßstäbe in ganz Europa an. In den frühen siebziger Jahren realisierte er in Mailand einen ersten Wohnblock. Dem folgten einige Schulprojekte (Broni, Fagnano und Ulani) und ein Friedhof in Modena. Entwurfsaktivitäten in den frühen achtziger Jahren reichten vom Möbeldesign bis zu städtebaulichen Konzeptionen. Rossi entwirft Projekte in den USA, Japan und Europa. 1988 gewinnt er den Wettbewerb für das Deutsche Historische Museum in Berlin. Der Kern in Rossis theoretischen Arbeiten ist der Typus. In ihm sind Entwurfstheorie und Praxis als Entlastungsstrategie vereint. Vom Typus bestimmte Formenmuster führen zu einer charakteristischen Ästhetik. So erklären sich etwa die harmonischen Stadtbilder vergangener Epochen aus dem Bautyp als Entwurfsprinzip. Rossis Interessen konzentrieren sich auf den Typus als zentrale Bauaufgabe in der Stadt (Teatro del Mondo, 1979) und Designobjekte der industriellen Produktion. Rossis Formensprache ist bestimmt durch symmetrische Bezüge – nach dem Muster geometrischer Idealstädte – und puristische Gestaltungselemente des italienischen Rationalismus der dreißiger Jahre. Bei seiner beharrlichen Beschäftigung mit den wesentlichen Elementen der Architektur entstehen Formen und Modelle, die beschwörend vor dem endgültigen Verlust des Typus warnen.

Aus dem breiten Spektrum der jüngeren Architektengeneration seien hier exemplarisch drei Namen genannt: Franco Stella, Francesco Venezia und Giorgio Grassi. Dem Venezianer Stella gelang 1975 bei einem Bürogebäude in Thiene/Vincenza durch Überlagerung dreier unterschiedlicher Raumsituationen eine glückliche Komposition. Venezia zeigt in seiner bildhauerischen Architektur – ähnlich wie der Deutsche Bienefeld – melancholische und geheimnisvolle Zeichen im Geiste Carlo Scarpas. Der Mailänder Grassi treibt Rossis Forderung nach Architekturreduktion zu einem monumentalen Klinkerpurismus.

SCHWEIZ

Die Schweiz ist aufgrund ihrer geographischen Lage und als Vielvölkerstaat das europäischste und zugleich ein kulturell geteiltes Land. Im deutschsprachigen Norden wird eine moderne Tradition fortgeführt, im Süden sind eher typologische Tendenzen zu beob-

intérêts de Rossi se concentrent sur le type comme mission architecturale centrale dans la ville (Teatro del Mondo 1979) et les objets design de la production industrielle. Le langage formel de Rossi est déterminé par des rapports symétriques – selon le modèle de villes idéales géométriques –, des éléments de représentation puristes et des typologies du rationalisme italien des années 30. De sa continuelle réflexion sur les éléments essentiels de l'architecture naissent des formes et des maquettes qui mettent instamment en garde contre la perte définitive du type.

Citons à titre d'exemple trois noms tirés du vaste éventail de la nouvelle génération d'architectes: Franco Stella, Francesco Venezia et Giorgio Grassi. Le Vénitien Stella a réussi en 1975 une heureuse composition en superposant trois espaces différents dans un bâtiment commercial à Thiene/Vicence. Dans son architecture plastique, Venezia montre – de même que l'Allemand Bienefeld – des signes mélancoliques et mystérieux dans l'esprit de Carlo Scarpa. Le Milanais Giorgio Grassi pousse l'exigence rossienne de réduction de l'architecture vers un purisme monumental en clinkers.

SUISSE

En raison de sa situation géographique et en tant qu'Etat multiracial, la Suisse est à la fois le pays le plus européen et un pays culturellement divisé. Dans le nord germanophone, on poursuit une tradition moderne. Au sud, on observe plutôt des tendances typologiques. Dans les années 20, l'architecte Hannes Meyer (1889–1954) fut le leader du modernisme suisse. Citons à titre d'exemple le bureau bâlois Diener & Diener comme représentant du néo-modernisme suisse.

Les architectes du Tessin italophone s'orientent selon les universités italiennes. Dans les années 80, l'Ecole tessinoise et son architecture de villas était qualifiée de »tuyau« dans les milieux architecturaux européens. On s'est particulièrement intéressé à Mario Botta, qui a étudié l'architecture aux Beaux-Arts de Milan. Ses variations géométriques sur le thème du cube ont attiré l'attention mondiale. Ivano Gianola, Livio Vacchini, Bruno Reichlin, Fabio Reinhart et Michael Alder sont également des représentants de l'Ecole tessinoise.

Luigi Snozzi est la plus grande autorité parmi les architectes de l'Ecole tessinoise. Son œuvre comprend quelques rares constructions, qui sont toutefois essentielles. Snozzi représente – à partir d'une conscience historique aiguë – la position de l'étude contextualiste. La force typologique de ses projets permet de reconnaître l'écriture d'un maître. Ses thèses sur la morphologie de la ville et ses réflexions

Mario Botta, Maison du Livre de l'Image et du Son, Villeurbanne, France,
1984–1988, south side (opposite page)
and view of skylight (above)

Luigi Snozzi, Diener House in Ronco/
Ascona, Switzerland, 1988–1989
(above)

Roger Diener, Gmurzynska Gallery in
Cologne, Germany, 1990–1991
(opposite page)

ition, while the South betrays more typological tendencies. The head of the Swiss Modern Movement in the twenties was Hannes Meyer (1898–1954). Representatives of contemporary neo-modernism include, for example, the Basle practice of Diener & Diener.

The architects from the Italian-speaking Ticino region are based around Italian universities. The Ticinese School, with its villa architecture, was considered something of an inside tip in European architectural circles in the eighties. Mario Botta, who studied architecture in Milan, attracted particular attention. His geometric variations upon the cube aroused international interest. Further members of the Ticinese School are Ivano Gianola, Livio Vacchini, Bruno Reichlin, Fabio Reinhart and Michael Alder.

Luigi Snozzi enjoys the greatest authority amongst the architects of the Ticinese School. His oeuvre runs to just a few, highly significant buildings. Snozzi argues for contextualized design, which he combines with his acute sense of history. The typological power of his

achten. In den zwanziger Jahren war Hannes Meyer (1889–1954) der führende Kopf der Schweizer Moderne. Als Vertreter der Neomoderne sei exemplarisch das Baseler Büro Diener & Diener genannt.

Die Architekten aus dem italienischsprachigen Tessin orientieren sich an den italienischen Universitäten. In den achtziger Jahren wurde die Tessiner Schule mit ihrer Villenarchitektur als Geheimtip in europäischen Architektenkreisen gehandelt. Großes Interesse galt besonders Mario Botta, seine geometrischen Variationen zum Thema Würfel erregten international Aufsehen. Weitere Vertreter der Tessiner Schule sind Ivano Gianola, Livio Vacchini, Bruno Reichlin, Fabio Reinhart und Michael Alder.

Größte Autorität unter den Architekten der Tessiner Schule genießt Luigi Snozzi. Sein Werk umfaßt einige wenige, doch recht bedeutende Bauten. Snozzi vertritt – aus einem geschärften Geschichtsbewußtsein heraus – die Position des kontextualistischen Entwurfs. Die typologische Kraft seiner Projekte läßt die Handschrift eines Meisters erkennen. Seine Thesen zur Mor-

politiques sur les conditions d'un urbanisme humain font de lui l'un des architectes européens les plus compétents.

AUTRICHE

En Autriche, les évolutions architecturales les plus remarquées se concentrent autour de Vienne. Les racines historiques de l'architecture actuelle remontent à Otto Wagner, Josef Hoffmann et Adolf Loos. Les deux chefs de file Gustav Peichl et Hans Hollein – d'une manière differente –, de même que le groupe Coop Himmelblau, exercent en Europe des influences très différentes.

Peichl parvient à l'apogée de sa carrière dans les années 70 avec ses studios pour la radio autrichienne (ORF) à Salzbourg, Linz et Innsbruck et un poste de communication à terre à Aflenz. Dans leur composition technique, ses constructions parlent le langage d'une esthétique mécanique. Avec sa station d'élimination de phosphates réalisée à Berlin-Tegel en 1986, qui est comparable aux projets industriels du muni-

Haus-Rucker-Co., »Wassereck«, 1976
(opposite page)

projects reveals the mark of a true master. His theories on the morphology of the city and his political reflection upon the conditions of human urban planning make him one of the most discerning architects in Europe.

AUSTRIA

Austria's most far-reaching architectural developments are largely concentrated within the Greater Vienna area. Contemporary architecture traces its historical roots back to Otto Wagner, Josef Hoffmann and Adolf Loos. The respectable figures of Gustav Peichl and Hans Hollein are both – albeit in very different ways – influential for Europe, as is the Coop Himmelblau group.

The height of Peichl's career came in the seventies, with his studios for Austrian State Radio (ORF) in Salzburg, Linz and Innsbruck and a ground signal station in Aflenz. The engineering-style composition of his buildings speaks the language of the machine aesthetic. He continued this line in 1968, with his Phosphate Elimination Works in Berlin-Tegel, comparable in quality to the industrial projects of Munich-based Kurt Ackermann. Although Peichl adapted his stylistic means in response to Post-Modernism, he also reacted to the movement with satirical cartoons under his pseudonym of »Ironimus«. For the Museum of Art in Bonn he used an iconological system in which the modern structure of the design is overlaid with a composition of post-modern cones. Even where Peichl's late works lack the avant-gardist impact of his buildings from the seventies, great weight is still attached to his opinion in architectural circles.

Hollein completed his first projects at the end of the sixties as an interior designer working in the style of Pop Art. Unwilling to restrict himself to an exclusively architectural career, he maintained the freedom to explore future ideas. He developed into an all-round designer of extraordinary creativity, and traditional architectural design forms only one area of his activities. It is little exaggeration to call Hollein one of Europe's most influential interior designers. His creative methods are unique in their use of signs and symbols. No other European architect has so successfully transformed the iconological theories of the seventies into reality. Hollein's most important work is the Abteiberg Museum in Mönchengladbach, completed in 1982 in collaboration with Thomas van den Valentyn, in which he achieves an ideal combination of interior qualities with external urban integration. The recently-completed Museum of Modern Art in Frankfurt, the competition for which Hollein won in 1982, is less convincing. After ten years of planning and construction work, the end product – richly or-

Hans Hollein, Museum of Modern Art in
Frankfurt/Main, Germany, 1982–1991

phologie der Stadt und seine politischen Reflexionen über die Bedingungen eines menschlichen Städtebaus machen ihn zu einem der urteilsfähigsten Architekten in Europa.

ÖSTERREICH

In Österreich konzentrieren sich die am meisten beachteten Architekturentwicklungen auf den Großraum Wien. Die geschichtlichen Wurzeln der aktuellen Architektur reichen bis zu den Urvätern Otto Wagner, Josef Hoffmann und Adolf Loos zurück. Europäischen Einfluß haben, auf ganz unterschiedliche Weise, die beiden Altmeister Gustav Peichl und Hans Hollein sowie die Gruppe Coop Himmelblau.

Peichl findet zum Höhepunkt seines Schaffens in den siebziger Jahren, mit seinen Studiobauten für den Österreichischen Rundfunk in Salzburg, Linz und Innsbruck und einer Erdfunkstation in Aflenz. Die Bauten sprechen in ihrer ingenieurmäßigen Komposition die Sprache einer Maschinenästhetik. Mit seiner Phosphateliminationsanlage in Berlin Tegel von 1986, die in ihrer Qualität mit Industrieprojekten des Münchners Kurt Ackermann zu vergleichen ist, hat er diese Entwurfslinie noch einmal fortgesetzt. Im Zeichen der Postmoderne verändert Peichl seine stilistischen Mittel, obwohl er als Karikaturist unter dem Pseudonym Ironimus, auch auf die Postmoderne mit spöttischen Skizzen reagiert hat. Beim Kunstmuseum in Bonn verwendet er ein ikonologisches System: Er überlagert die moderne Struktur des Entwurfs mit einer Komposition postmoderner Kegel. Auch wenn Peichls Spätwerk nicht mehr die avantgardistische Kraft seiner Bauten aus den siebziger Jahren besitzt, ist sein Urteil immer noch von großem Gewicht.

Hollein realisiert seine ersten Projekte Ende der sechziger Jahre als Innenarchitekt im Stil der Pop Art. Auf eine einengende Architektenlaufbahn will er sich nicht festlegen und bewahrt so Spielraum für seine künftigen Ideen. Er entwickelte sich zu einem Allround-Designer von außerordentlicher Kreativität, für den der traditionelle architektonische Entwurf nur einen Teil seiner Aktivitäten ausmacht. Es ist kaum übertrieben, Hollein als einen der einflußreichsten Innenarchitekten Europas zu bezeichnen. Das Besondere seiner schöpferischen Methode ist das Entwerfen über Zeichen und Symbole. Kein anderer europäischer Architekt hat wie Hollein die ikonologischen Theorien der siebziger Jahre in die Praxis umgesetzt. Sein bedeutendstes Bauwerk ist das Städtische Museum auf dem Abteiberg in Mönchengladbach, das er 1982 unter Mitwirkung des deutschen Architekten Thomas van den Valentyn realisierte. Hier gelingt es ihm in idealer Weise, innenräumliche Qualitäten mit einer städtebaulich gelungenen Architektur zu verbinden. Das

chois Kurt Ackermann du point de vue qualité, il a une fois encore poursuivi cette ligne d'étude. Sous le signe du postmodernisme, Peichl varie ses moyens stylistiques, bien qu'il ait également fait des caricatures se moquant du postmodernisme sous le pseudonyme de Ironimus. Pour le Musée de l'art à Bonn, il emploie un système iconologique: il superpose la structure moderne du projet à une composition de cônes postmodernes. Même si l'œuvre tardif de Peichl ne possède plus la force avant-gardiste de ses constructions des années 70, son opinion pèse toujours lourd dans les milieux architecturaux.

Hollein réalise à la fin des années 60 ses premiers projets dans le style du Pop Art en tant qu'ensemblier. Il ne veut pas se fixer sur une carrière d'architecte restrictive et conserve ainsi une marge pour ses idées futures. Il est devenu un designer polyvalent d'une extraordinaire créativité pour qui le projet architectonique traditionnel ne représente qu'une partie de ses activités. Il est à peine exagéré de dire que Hollein est l'un des ensembliers les plus influents d'Europe. L'originalité de sa méthode créatrice est de projeter à l'aide de signes et de symboles. Aucun autre architecte européen n'a mis en pratique les théories iconologiques des années 70 comme Hollein. Son édifice le plus significatif est le Musée municipal sur l'Abteiberg, à Mönchengladbach, qu'il a réalisé en 1982 en collaboration avec l'architecte allemand Thomas van den Valentyn. Dans ce projet, il parvient de manière idéale à allier des qualités intérieures à une architecture urbanistiquement réussie. Le Musée de l'art moderne de Francfort, que Hollein a récemment terminé après

Gustav Peichl, Kunstforum Wien,
Austria, 1988–1989

namented with post-modern accessories – already seems a relic of past times.

Alongside Haus-Rucker-Co. and Missing Link, Coop Himmelblau numbers amongst the most important utopianist groups of the generation of '68. Wolf D. Prix and Helmut Swiczinsky founded an office for experimental architecture in 1968. The philosophy behind their architecture originated in the rebellious mentality of their generation, which expressed its criticism of the system in a variety of ways, not least by aesthetic and architectural means. Coop Himmelblau found stylistic expression appropriate to their ideas in arthropomorphic architecture in the late sixties and in deconstruction twenty years later.

Coop Himmelblau attracted international attention in 1985 with an entirely open geometry expressing a view of the times shared by more than just the young generation. It thereby took a stand against a Post-Modernism grown painful, a Post-Modernism appropriated and abused by industry and unable to prevent the scenario of the »chaos city«. Deconstruction solves no problems, either; at best, it draws attention to them. Neither does it repair cities or offer strategies for an economic and technically skilful creation of space. It concentrates instead upon a puzzle game of spatial and constructive possibilities, on creating surprises. But it is precisely the counter-innovation represented by the manipulation of such bizarre design elements which offers architects a new possibility of escape from their dead end.

SCANDINAVIA

Scandinavian architectural activity was formerly dominated by such personalities as Arne Jacobsen and Alvar Aalto. Two Scandinavian architects have also gained international fame with their spectacular designs: Jørn Utzon, with his expressive 1956 Sydney Opera House, on which project the young Spanish architect Rafael Moneo also worked, and von Spreckelsen, with his 1987 design for the Arche de la Défense which implements the utopian vision of El Lissitzky's »Cloud Stirrup«. Thanks to its outlying position, Scandinavia escapes the rapid fluctuations of avant-garde trends. As in the Netherlands, its stability guarantees high general artistic and technological standards of architecture. Its well-preserved historical buildings have also served to ensure orderly architectural development. It is no accident that the overall thread running through Scandinavian architecture of the last decades is one of classicism with a tendency towards classical Modernism. Alongside interesting experiments with the readily-available material of wood, the scene is also dominated by sober modern and – less frequently – post-modern structures.

kürzlich fertiggestellte Museum für Moderne Kunst in Frankfurt, das Hollein 1982 als Wettbewerb gewann, weiß weniger zu überzeugen. Die genaue Umsetzung des Entwurfs mit reichem Schmuck postmoderner Versatzstücke erweckt nach zehn Jahren Planung und Bauzeit den Eindruck, Relikt einer bereits überholten Zeit zu sein.

Von den utopistischen Gruppen der 68er-Generation ist neben Haus-Rucker-Co und Missing Link besonders Coop Himmelblau zu nennen. Wolf D. Prix und Helmut Swiczinsky gründeten 1968 ein Büro für experimentelle Architektur. Die Grundidee ihrer Architektur entspringt dem Verweigerungsgedanken der damaligen Generation, die ihre Kritik auf verschiedene Weise – darunter auch mit ästhetischen und architektonischen Mitteln – äußerte. Coop Himmelblaus Intentionen fanden Ende der sechziger Jahre in der arthropomorphen Architektur und zwanzig Jahre später in der Dekonstruktion ihren jeweils angemessenen stilistischen Ausdruck.

Internationale Aufmerksamkeit gewinnt Coop Himmelblau 1985 mit einer völlig offenen Geometrie, die das Zeitgefühl nicht nur der jungen Generation ausdrückt. Diesmal geht es um den Widerstand gegen eine peinlich gewordene Postmoderne, die von der Industrie vereinnahmt und verbraucht wird und das Chaos »Stadt« nicht verhindern kann. Die Dekonstruktion löst indes keine Probleme, sondern macht diese – bestenfalls – bewußt. Sie repariert keine Städte, bietet keine Strategie zur wirtschaftlichen und statisch geschickten Realisierung von Raum. Statt dessen konzentriert sie sich auf ein Verwirrspiel räumlicher und konstruktiver Möglichkeiten, auf Überraschungseffekte. Aber gerade die Inszenierung solcher bizarren Gestaltungsmöglichkeiten als Gegeninnovation ist das neue Prinzip Hoffnung, das die Architekten aus einer Sackgasse führen soll.

SKANDINAVIEN

Das skandinavische Architekturgeschehen war einst dominiert von Persönlichkeiten wie Arne Jacobsen und Alvar Aalto. Im übrigen sind skandinavische Architekten mit spektakulären Entwürfen international zweimal hervorgetreten: Jørn Utzon 1956 mit seinem expressiven Entwurf für die Oper in Sydney, an dem auch der Spanier Rafael Moneo als junger Architekt mitgearbeitet hat, sowie von Spreckelsen 1987 mit seiner Arche de la Défense, der die utopische Idee von Lissitzkys Wolkenbügel verwirklicht. Skandinavien ist durch seine Randlage nicht den Wechselbädern avantgardistischer Strömungen ausgesetzt. Diese Beständigkeit garantiert, ähnlich wie in den Niederlanden, eine hohe gestalterische und technologische Durchschnittsqualität der Architektur. Dane-

avoir remporté le concours en 1982, est moins convaincant. La transposition exacte du projet avec une riche ornementation de décorations postmodernes donne l'impression, au bout de dix ans de planification et de construction, d'être un vestige d'une époque déjà dépassée.

Parmi les groupes utopiques de la génération de 68, il convient de citer d'abord, outre Haus-Rucker-Co et Missing Link, Coop Himmelblau. Wolf D. Prix et Helmut Swiczinsky ont fondé en 1968 un bureau d'architecture expérimentale. L'idée de base de leur architecture provient de l'idée de refus de la génération de l'époque, qui exprimait sa critique de diverses manières, entre autres avec des moyens esthétiques et architectoniques. Les idées de Coop Himmelblau ont trouvé leur expression stylistique appropriée à la fin des années 60 dans l'architecture anthropomorphe et, vingt ans plus tard, dans la déconstruction.

Coop Himmelblau a attiré l'attention internationale en 1985 avec une géométrie totalement ouverte qui n'exprime pas seulement la notion de temps de la jeune génération. Cette fois, il s'agit de l'opposition à un postmodernisme devenu embarrassant, qui est revendiqué et usé par l'industrie et ne peut empêcher le »chaos de la ville«. La déconstruction ne résout aucun problème, mais les rend – tout au plus – conscients. Elle ne répare pas les villes, n'offre aucune stratégie pour la réalisation économique et statiquement adroite d'espace. Au lieu de cela, elle se concentre sur une confusion de possibilités spatiales et constructives, sur des effets de surprise. Mais l'orchestration de réalisations bizarres en tant que contre-innovation est justement le nouveau principe de l'espoir qui doit sortir les architectes de l'impasse.

SCANDINAVIE

La scène architecturale scandinave était autrefois dominée par des personnalités telles que Arne Jacobsen et Alvar Aalto. Les architectes scandinaves se sont au reste distingués par deux fois à l'échelon international avec des projets spectaculaires: Jørn Utzon en 1956, avec son projet expressif pour l'opéra de Sydney auquel le jeune architecte espagnol Rafael Moneo a également participé; de même que von Spreckelsen en 1987, avec son Arche de La Défense, qui réalise l'idée utopique des »Arc-Nuages« de Lissitzky. De par sa situation limitrophe, la Scandinavie n'est pas exposée aux variations des tendances avant-gardistes. Cette constance garantit, tout comme aux Pays-Bas, une haute qualité moyenne de l'architecture au point de vue création et technologie. A côté, le nombre de constructions historiques bien conservées a maintenu l'ordre dans les développements architectoniques. Ce n'est pas un hasard si le classicisme

Hans Dissing, Otto Weitling, Kunstsammlung Nordrhein-Westfalen in
Düsseldorf, Germany, 1976–1986
(above)

Arne Kjaer, Claus Kristensen, Kaas
Staalbyg Head Office in Pandrup,
Denmark, 1989 (opposite page)

For the Danish architecture exhibition at Odense in 1989, the young architect generation armed itself from the formal arsenal of Post-Modernism. In practice, however, the trend is towards sleeker, landscape-related forms revealing little inclination toward experiment, as illustrated by the holiday estate in Ebeltoft, by Knud Friis and Elmar Moltke.

In 1975 Hans Dissing and Otto Weitling took over Arne Jacobsen's practice. In 1976 they won the competition for the Kunstsammlung Nordrhein-Westfalen for which Stirling had also submitted a design – a forerunner for his later Stuttgart museum. The Kunstsammlung, one of the best new museum buildings in Europe, proves that variations upon the style of classical Modernism have been far from exhausted.

To judge from the 1990 architecture exhibition in Malmö, Sweden and Norway have fewer surprises to offer. The classicism of such as Sigurd Lewerentz and Klas Anselm is outdated, but has yet to be replaced by truly new perspectives. Lewerentz and Anselm completed a number of impressive buildings after the Sec-

ben hat der gut erhaltene historische Baubestand Ordnung in den architektonischen Entwicklungen bewahrt. Nicht zufällig ist der Klassizismus mit Tendenzen zur klassischen Moderne der rote Faden, der sich durch die gesamte skandinavische Architektur der letzten Jahrzehnte zieht. Neben interessanten Experimenten mit dem reichlich vorhandenen Baustoff Holz dominieren nüchtern-moderne und wenige postmoderne Bauten auch die aktuelle skandinavische Architekturszene.

Auf der dänischen Bauausstellung in Odense 1989 bedient sich die junge Architektengeneration aus dem Formenarsenal der Postmoderne. In der Praxis überwiegen jedoch schlichtere, landschaftsbezogene Formtendenzen, die wenig Neigung zu Experimenten offenbaren. Die Feriensiedlung in Ebeltoft von Knud Friis und Elmar Moltke ist dafür ein überzeugendes Beispiel.

1975 übernehmen die Architekten Hans Dissing und Otto Weitling das Büro von Arne Jacobsen. 1976 gewinnen sie den Wettbewerb für die Kunstsammlung

est, avec des tendances au modernisme classique, le fil conducteur qui traverse toute l'architecture scandinave des dernières décennies. A côté d'expériences intéressantes avec le bois qui abonde, les constructions modernes et quelques constructions postmodernes dominent sobrement la scène architecturale scandinave actuelle.

A l'occasion de l'exposition danoise de la construction à Odense en 1989, la jeune génération d'architectes se sert de l'arsenal formel du postmodernisme. Dans la pratique, les tendances formelles plus simples se rapportant au paysage et ne tendant guère aux expériences, l'emportent toutefois. Le village de vacances de Ebeltoft, conçu par Knud Friis et Elmar Moltke, en est un exemple convaincant.

En 1975, les architectes Hans Dissing et Otto Weitling reprennent le bureau d'Arne Jacobsen. En 1976, ils gagnent le concours pour la collection d'objets d'art de Rhénanie-Westphalie, auquel James Stirling a également participé avec un précurseur du musée de Stuttgart. Dans ce bâtiment, qui fait partie des meil-

Kari Niskasaari, Jorma Öhman, look-
out tower in Oulu, Finland, 1989
(opposite page)

Kari Kuosma, Esko Valkama, terrace
house at the Nordform '90 exposition in
Malmö, Sweden, 1990

ond World War in the tradition of Gunnar Asplund. An exceptional position is occupied in Sweden by the English-born Ralph Erskine, who has found his own style of spontaneous and expressive architecture. His housing development in Newcastle-upon-Tyne (1969—1980) attracted world-wide attention. From today's standpoint, his dramatic expressionism appears a reaction to the bloodless schematism of the late Modernism of the seventies. Some critics see in him a forerunner of contemporary deconstruction. Erskine's work has had little influence in Scandinavia, however. His style has clearly changed in the last few years: his architecture is today more closely based on Russian Constructivism.

Finland has seen the growth of an architecture whose roots lie in the development of the autonomous state. The »Helsinki School« is formally influenced by Le Corbusier, Aalto, Lewerentz and Ivan Leonidov. An example here is the Kristian Gullichsen, Erkki Kairamo & Timo Vormala partnership. Gullichsen laconically describes his passion for quotations as a »love of clichés – but only the best«. Thus, despite his obvious borrowings from the past, he achieves a convincingly contemporary interpretation of Modernism. The »School of Oulu« has quite different aims, attempting a symbiosis of national romanticism with regional architecture and landscape. Inspired by Rudolf Steiner, one of its important teachers, Reima Pietilä, seeks to

Knud Friis, Elmar Moltke, holiday estate in Ebeltoft, Denmark, 1987–1988

in Nordrhein-Westfalen, an dem auch James Stirling mit einem Vorläufer für das Museum in Stuttgart teilgenommen hat. Bei diesem Gebäude, das zu den besten neuen Museen Europas gehört, zeigen Dissing und Weitling, daß Varianten im Stil der klassischen Moderne noch nicht erschöpft sind.

In Schweden und Norwegen ist – nach der Bauausstellung 1990 in Malmö zu urteilen – wenig Überraschendes zu beobachten. Der Klassizismus von Sigurd Lewerentz oder Klas Anselm ist überholt, aber nicht durch wirklich neue Perspektiven ersetzt worden. Lewerentz und Anselm hatten nach dem Zweiten Weltkrieg in der Nachfolge Gunnar Asplunds einige beeindruckende Bauten realisiert. Eine Ausnahmeerscheinung in Schweden ist der gebürtige Engländer Ralph Erskine, der mit seiner spontanen und expressiven Architektur einen eigenen stilistischen Weg gefunden hat. Besonders mit seinem Wohnprojekt in Newcastle-Upon-Tyne (1969–1980) erregte er weltweit Aufmerksamkeit. Sein dramatischer Expressionismus erscheint aus heutiger Sicht als Opposition gegen den Schematismus der ausgebluteten Spätmoderne in den siebziger Jahren. Einige Kritiker sehen in ihm einen Vorläufer der aktuellen Dekonstruktion. Erskines Werk hat jedoch in Skandinavien wenig Wirkung gezeigt. Sein Stil hat sich in den letzten Jahren deutlich verändert: Seine Architektur bezieht sich heute mehr auf den russischen Konstruktivismus.

In Finnland hat sich eine Architektur ausgebildet, deren Identität ihre Wurzeln in der Entwicklung des autonomen Staates hat. Die »Helsinki-Schule« ist formal geprägt von Le Corbusier, Aalto, Lewerentz und Iwan Leonidow. Beispielhaft ist hier das Büro Kristian Gullichsen, Erkki Kairamo & Timo Vormala zu erwähnen. Lakonisch bezeichnet Gullichsen seine große Passion für Zitate als »Liebe zu den Klischees – aber nur den besten«. So gelangt er trotz seiner überdeutlichen Anlehnung an Vorbilder zu einer überzeugend aktuellen Interpretation der Moderne. Ganz anders die Ansätze der »Schule von Oulu«. Hier wird konsequent eine Symbiose des nationalen Romantizismus mit regionaler Architektur und Landschaft angestrebt. Als Lehrer ist Reima Pietilä zu nennen, der – von Rudolf Steiner inspiriert – versucht, die Tradition des klassischen Funktionalismus mit Formen der Natur zu verknüpfen. Sein Schüler Lauri Louekari geht weiter. Dessen organische Architektur verknüpft den traditionellen Klassizismus mit der regionalen Holzbauweise und fügt sie in die Landschaft ein.

SPANIEN

Seit Mitte der sechziger Jahre ist Spanien das klassische Urlaubsland für die Industrieländer Mitteleuropas. Zehn Jahre später überzieht ein gewaltiger Bau-

leurs musées européens récents, Dissing et Weitling montrent que les variantes dans le style du modernisme classique ne sont pas encore épuisées.

En Suède et en Norvège, on note peu de surprises après l'exposition de la construction de 1990 à Malmö. Le classicisme de Sigurd Lewerentz ou de Klas Anselm est dépassé, mais pas remplacé par des perspectives vraiment nouvelles. Lewerentz et Anselm avaient réalisé quelques bâtiments impressionnants après la Deuxième Guerre mondiale à l'exemple de Gunnar Asplund. L'Anglais Ralph Erskine, qui a trouvé sa propre voie stylistique avec son architecture spontanée et expressive, est un phénomène exceptionnel en Suède. Il a attiré l'attention mondiale, particulièrement avec son projet d'habitation à Newcastle-upon-Tyne (1969–1980). Son expressionnisme dramatique fait aujourd'hui figure d'opposition au schématisme du modernisme tardif saigné à blanc dans les années 70. Quelques critiques voient en lui un précurseur de l'actuelle déconstruction. L'œuvre d'Erskine n'a cependant guère eu d'effet en Scandinavie. Son style a nettement changé au cours des dernières années: son architecture se rapporte aujourd'hui davantage au constructivisme russe.

Une architecture, dont l'identité a sa racine dans le développement du pays autonome, s'est formée en Finlande. L'Ecole d'Helsinki est formellement marquée par Le Corbusier, Aalto, Lewerentz et Ivan Leonidov. Citons à titre d'exemple le bureau Kristian Gullichsen, Erkki Kairamo & Timo Vormala. Gullichsen qualifie laconiquement sa grande passion pour les citations d'»amour des clichés – mais seulement des meilleurs«. Bien qu'il s'appuie excessivement sur des modèles, il parvient à une interprétation tout à fait actuelle du modernisme. Il en va tout différemment de l'Ecole d'Oulu. Celle-ci vise de manière conséquente une symbiose du romantisme national avec l'architecture et le paysage régionaux. Citons Reima Pietilä comme professeur – inspiré par Rudolf Steiner –, qui tente d'allier la tradition du fonctionnalisme classique aux formes de la nature. Son élève Lauri Louekari va encore plus loin: son architecture organique unit de manière convaincante le classicisme traditionnel et la construction en bois régionale et l'insère dans le paysage.

ESPAGNE

Depuis le milieu des années 60, l'Espagne est le lieu de vacances classique des pays industrialisés d'Europe centrale. Dix ans plus tard, l'essor prodigieux de la construction s'empare des longues côtes méditerranéennes et fait dans les sites des ravages d'une ampleur jusque-là inconnue. Le moteur de l'architecture, l'économie de marché, se montre de son côté le

Santiago Calatrava, Arnold Amsler,
Werner Rüegger, Stadelhofen Train
Station, Zurich, Switzerland, 1985–1990
(above and opposite page)

fuse the traditions of classical functionalism with the forms of nature. His pupil Lauri Louekari goes even further. His organic architecture convincingly combines traditional classicism with regional wood-building methods and integrates the whole into the surrounding landscape.

SPAIN

In the mid-sixties Spain emerged as the standard holiday destination for the industrial nations of Central Europe. Ten years later its Mediterranean coastline was swept by a huge building boom which devastated the landscape on a previously unknown scale; the market economy, driving force of architecture, showed its ugliest and most dangerous face. Nowhere in Europe is the difficulty of marrying liberality with culture in the field of building more apparent. High artistic standards are set both by Spain's rich architectural heritage and by the contemporary architecture which has commanded international respect since the eighties.

boom die langen Mittelmeerküsten und richtet land-
schaftsräumliche Verwüstungen in bisher unbekann-
tem Ausmaß an. Der Architekturmotor Marktwirtschaft zeigt sich hier von seiner häßlichsten und ge-
fährlichsten Seite. Nirgendwo in Europa wird die
Schwierigkeit so deutlich, das Prinzip Liberalität mit
dem Prinzip Baukultur in Einklang zu bringen. Maßstäbe hoher Baukultur bietet das reiche historische
Architekturerbe Spaniens ebenso wie die aktuelle Architektur, die seit den achtziger Jahren international
Beachtung findet.

Eine sehr zurückhaltende Architekturentwicklung läßt
nach dem Krieg und während der Franco-Ära wenig
Spielraum für modische Auswüchse der späten Moderne. Auch die nachfolgende Postmoderne zeigt,
von den Bauten Ricardo Bofills einmal abgesehen,
keine starke Ausprägung. Nach dem Tod Francos im
Jahre 1975 setzt eine Intellektualisierung der Architektur ein, die sich exemplarisch in frühen Arbeiten von
Lluís Clotet und Oscar Tusquets sowie von Antonio
Cruz und Antonio Ortiz zeigt. Beeinflußt von der mit-

plus laid et le plus dangereux. Nulle part en Europe on
ne voit aussi nettement combien il est difficile de
concilier le principe de la libéralité et le principe de la
culture architecturale. Le riche héritage architectural
de l'Espagne et l'architecture actuelle, qui est considérée avec beaucoup d'attention dans le monde entier depuis les années 80, offrent tous les critères d'une
grande culture architecturale.

Après la guerre et pendant l'ère franquiste, une évolution architecturale plutôt réservée laisse peu de
marge pour les excès en vogue du modernisme tardif.
Le postmodernisme qui s'ensuit n'est pas très prononcé, à l'exception des constructions de Ricardo
Bofill. Après la mort de Franco, en 1975, s'instaure
une intellectualisation de l'architecture qui se manifeste de manière exemplaire dans les œuvres de début de Lluís Clotet et d'Oscar Tusquets, d'Antonio
Cruz et d'Antonio Ortiz. Le potentiel d'une architecture symbolique subtile se développe à partir de la fin
des années 70 sous l'influence de la discussion idéale
et théorique en Europe centrale. Les architectes espa-

Juan Navarro Baldeweg, Hydraulics
Museum in Murcia, Spain, 1983–1988
(above)

Jordi Garcés, Enric Soria, Picasso
Museum in Barcelona, Spain,
1981–1986 (opposite page)

Spain's very conservative architectural development
after the war and during the Franco era left little room
for fashionable Modernist excesses. The Post-Modernism which followed was – Ricardo Bofill aside –
similarly unremarkable. The intellectualization of architecture which began after Franco's death in 1975 is
reflected in the early works of Lluís Clotet and Oscar
Tusquets and in works by Antonio Cruz and Antonio
Ortiz. Influenced by the Central European discussion
of theory and model, a symbolic and sensitive architecture began to emerge as from the late seventies.
Spanish architects ventured confident experiments
with the forms of Modernism, with leading roles being
taken by Rafael Moneo from Madrid and the Barcelona partnership of Josep Martorell, Oriol Bohigas
and David Mackay. Ricardo Bofill, with his dramatic
interpretation of Post-Modernism, and Santiago
Calatrava, with his organically associative constructions, are particularly well-known in Europe. The
Spanish scene nevertheless has much more to offer.
Mention should be made of Juan Navarro Baldeweg

teleuropäischen Leitbild- und Theoriediskussion, entfaltet sich ab den späten siebziger Jahren das Potential einer zeichenhaften und feinsinnigen Architektur. Spanische Architekten wagen souveräne Experimente mit den Formen der Moderne, wobei Rafael Moneo aus Madrid und der Architektengruppe Josep Martorell, Oriol Bohigas und David Mackay aus Barcelona eine führende Rolle zuzusprechen ist. In Mitteleuropa sind Bofill mit seiner dramatischen Umsetzung der Postmoderne und Santiago Calatrava mit organisch-assoziativen Konstruktionen besonders bekannt geworden. Aber die spanische Szene hat noch viel mehr zu bieten.

Namentlich zu erwähnen sind beispielsweise Juan Navarro Baldeweg (Hydraulisches Museum, Murcia, 1988), Jaume Bach mit Gabriel Mora (Weinschule in Sant Sadurni D'Anoia, 1988), Jordi Garcés mit Enric Soria (Wissenschaftsmuseum, Barcelona, 1980) und Eduard Bru mit Josep Lluís Mateo (Institut Marti i Pol, Barcelona, 1983). Der Garten der Villa Cecilia in Sarria, Barcelona (1986) von J. A. Martínez Lapeña und

gnols osent des expériences spontanées avec les formes du modernisme, à l'occasion de quoi il convient d'attribuer un rôle de leader à Rafael Moneo de Madrid et au groupe Josep Martorell, Oriol Bohigas et David Mackay de Barcelone. Ricardo Bofill et sa transposition dramatique du postmodernisme, Santiago Calatrava et ses constructions organico-associatives ont acquis une grande réputation en Europe centrale. Mais la scène espagnole a encore beaucoup plus à offrir.

Il convient de citer par exemple Juan Navarro Baldeweg (Musée hydraulique, Murcie, 1988), Jaume Bach avec Gabriel Mora (Ecole d'oenologie, Sant Sadurni D'Anoia, 1988), Jordi Garcés avec Enric Soria (Musée de la science, Barcelone, 1980), Eduard Bru avec Josep Lluís Mateo (Institut Marti i Pol, Barcelone, 1983). Le jardin de la Villa Cecilia à Sarria, Barcelone (1986) de J. A. Martínez Lapeña et Elias Torres Tur manifeste une surprenante féerie dans le style d'un modernisme surréel. En raison du climat et comme lieux de communication, le jardin et l'espace urbain

(Hydraulic Museum, Murcia, 1988), Jaume Bach with Gabriel Mora (Viticultural College, Sant Sadurni d'Anoia, 1988), Jordi Garcés with Enric Soria (Science Museum, Barcelona, 1980) and Eduard Bru with Josep Lluís Mateo (Marti i Pol Institute, Barcelona, 1983). The Villa Cecilia garden (1986) in Sarria, Barcelona, by J. A. Martínez Lapeña and Elias Torres Tur, is characterized by a surprising fantasticality in the style of a Surrealist Modernism. Both due to the climate and as places of communication, gardens and urban spaces enjoy a higher status in Spain than in Central Europe. Hence the considerable architectural effort devoted to recent piazza designs, such as the Plaza de Sants in Barcelona by Albert Viaplana and Helio Piñón (1981–1983). But even sleepy backwaters can reveal squares whose design might well serve as a model for other European nations.

The stylistic deployment of deconstruction remains confined in Spain to buildings and open spaces whose standard far exceeds that of comparable commissions and themes in Central Europe. The architecture of the young Spanish avant-garde may be generally located somewhere between tradition, symbolism and neo-Modernism, an architecture of »New Sensuousness« displaying a remarkable creativity.

PORTUGAL

Alvaro Siza is Portugal's internationally best-known architect. Committed to the expressive means of regional architecture, he uses modest commissions through which to develop his own modern formal idiom. With its simple geometry and reduction of materials, his architecture recalls such projects of classical Modernism as the houses in the Stuttgart Weissenhof estate by Le Corbusier, Bruno Taut and Mies van der Rohe. Siza adds new elements with a Mediterranean flavour, which are perhaps derived from the popular architecture of Portuguese housing developments. Siza's strength lies in his bridging of the gap between the sophisticated architecture of the Mediterranean villa and the sparse aesthetic of mass housing structures. It is precisely this ability to combine public commission with formal experimentation which makes Siza's work so important. Siza's stylistically most developed project is the 1982 Borges and Irmao Bank in Villa de Condo. Notable buildings abroad include the Schlesische Torhaus in Berlin (1980) and two residential houses in The Hague (1986).

With the approach of the twenty-first century, the dream and the reality of the architectural aesthetic are drifting ever further apart. The increasingly critical tastes of our consumer society leave the architect helpless in the face of the advancing destruction of

Alvaro Siza, Schlesisches Torhaus in Berlin, Germany, 1980–1983

Elias Torres Tur zeigt eine überraschende Märchenhaftigkeit im Stile einer surrealen Moderne. Garten und Stadtraum haben in Spanien – allein schon vom Klima her und als Ort der Kommunikation – einen anderen Stellenwert als in Mitteleuropa. Dies erklärt die beachtlichen architektonischen Leistungen bei neueren Platzgestaltungen. Als Beispiel sei die Plaza de Sants in Barcelona von Albert Viaplana und Helio Piñón (1981–1983) genannt. Aber selbst verträumte kleine Ortschaften überraschen immer wieder mit gestalteten Plätzen, die für andere europäische Nationen Vorbild sein könnten.

Der stilistische Einsatz der Dekonstruktion bleibt in Spanien auf Objekte und Freidächer beschränkt, die in ihrem Niveau vergleichbare Aufgaben und Themen in Mitteleuropa weit übertreffen. Insgesamt zeigt die junge spanische Avantgarde eine zeichenhafte Architektur zwischen Tradition, Symbolismus und Neomoderne, eine Architektur der »Neuen Sinnlichkeit« von außerordentlicher Kreativität.

PORTUGAL

Der international bekannteste Architekt Portugals ist Alvaro Siza. Den Ausdrucksmitteln einer regionalen Architektur verbunden, entwickelt er am Beispiel kleiner Bauaufgaben eine eigene moderne Formensprache. Mit ihrer einfachen Geometrie und der Reduktion der Materialien erinnert seine Architektur an Projekte der klassischen Moderne, beispielsweise an die Häuser der Stuttgarter Weißenhofsiedlung von Le Corbusier, Bruno Taut und Mies van der Rohe. Siza fügt neue Elemente mediterranen Charakters hinzu, die ihren Ursprung vielleicht im volksarchitektonischen Siedlungsbau Portugals haben. Sizas Stärke liegt darin, Brücken zu schlagen zwischen den feinsinnigen Experimenten mediterraner Villenbauten und der sparsam pointierten Ästhetik des Massenwohnungsbaus. Gerade diese Fähigkeit, gesellschaftliche Aufgaben mit Formexperimenten glücklich zu verbinden, macht die Arbeit Sizas bedeutend. Das stilistisch ausgeprägteste Projekt Sizas ist die Borges und Irmao Bank in Villa de Condo, Portugal, von 1982. Von seinen Bauten im Ausland sind besonders das Schlesische Torhaus in Berlin (1980) und zwei Wohnhäuser in Den Haag (1986) zu erwähnen.

Wunsch und Wirklichkeit architektonischer Ästhetik entfernen sich zunehmend mit der Annäherung an das 21. Jahrhundert. Einem durch Warenästhetik geschärften Blick der Gesellschaft steht die Ohnmacht der Architekten gegenüber: Unübersehbar ist die fortschreitende Zerstörung gewachsener Städte durch den Innovationsdruck der Moderne und den Verlust des Typus.

n'ont pas la même valeur dans la discussion politique en Espagne et en Europe centrale. Ceci explique les réalisations architectoniques appréciables dans les récents aménagements de places. Citons par exemple la Plaza de Sants à Barcelone, réalisée par Albert Viaplana et Helio Piñón (1981–1983). Même les petites localités surprennent toujours avec leurs places aménagées qui pourraient servir de modèle aux autres nations européennes.

En Espagne, l'intervention stylistique de la déconstruction demeure limitée à des objets et à des toits qui surpassent de loin, de par leur niveau, les tâches et les thèmes comparables en Europe centrale. Dans l'ensemble, la jeune avant-garde espagnole présente une architecture symbolique entre la tradition, le symbolisme et le néo-modernisme, une architecture de la »nouvelle sensibilité« extraordinairement créative.

PORTUGAL

L'architecte portugais le plus connu à l'échelon international est Alvaro Siza. Relié aux moyens d'expression d'une architecture régionale, il développe, suivant l'exemple de petites constructions, un langage formel moderne qui lui est propre. Avec sa géométrie simple et sa réduction des matériaux, son architecture rappelle les projets du modernisme classique, par exemple les maisons construites par Le Corbusier, Bruno Taut et Mies van der Rohe dans la Weißenhofsiedlung à Stuttgart. Siza ajoute de nouveaux éléments de caractère méditerranéen, qui tirent peut-être leur origine des lotissements populaires du Portugal. La force de Siza consiste à jeter des ponts entre les expériences subtiles des villas méditerranéennes et l'esthétique discrètement soulignée de l'habitat de masse. C'est justement cette aptitude à relier heureusement des problèmes sociaux à des expériences formelles qui rend significatif le travail de Siza. La Borges & Irmao Bank à Villa de Condo, Portugal, réalisée en 1982, est le projet de Siza qui est le plus marqué du point de vue style. Parmi ses bâtiments construits à l'étranger, signalons la maison-porche de Silésie à Berlin (1980) et deux maisons d'habitation à La Haye (1986).

Désir et réalité d'esthétique architectonique s'éloignent de plus en plus au fur et à mesure qu'approche le XXIe siècle. L'impuissance des architectes s'oppose au regard de la société aiguisé par l'esthétique des marchandises: la destruction progressive des villes, qui se sont développées sous la pression innovative du modernisme et la perte du type, est incontestable. Cette contradiction non éliminable entre la production et la réception de l'esthétique reflète d'une manière cachée un autre problème fondamental: l'erreur

historically mature cities – destruction caused by ceaseless modernist innovation and the loss of type. The irreconcilable contradiction between aesthetic production and aesthetic reception points to another fundamental problem: Modernism as an ecological error. Since the beginning of the century, the architecture of our technocratic society has been heading towards an evolutionary dead end.

The most momentous political event accompanying the start of the modern movement was the Russian Revolution. The idealistic visions and the broad spectrum of an ecstatic aesthetic which is released in architecture, continue to inspire architects today. The avant-garde of those times was convinced that the world could be shaped to its own ideas and that architecture would start off along a new path. That path turned into an odyssey, and every generation of architects since has experienced a similar succession of aesthetic highs and lows.

Searching for the origin and meaning of their inherited aesthetic, architects of the new generation have now, at the start of the nineties, arrived back at the very point from which their forefathers set off along the original path: the age of classical Modernism. This – secret – renaissance explains the newly rekindled enthusiasm for Le Corbusier, Leonidov and El Lissitzky. Young architects are now seeking to design in the spirit of classical Modernism and to reach at last the goal which eluded their ancestors: the final accomplishment of Modernism.

Enric Miralles, Carme Pinós, Parets
Roofing in Barcelona, Spain, 1985

Dieser unaufhebbare Widerspruch zwischen Produktion und Rezeption der Ästhetik spiegelt auf verborgene Weise ein anderes fundamentales Problem wider: den ökologischen Irrtum der Moderne. Seit Beginn dieses Jahrhunderts droht auch die Architektur einer technokratischen Gesellschaft in eine entwicklungsgeschichtliche Sackgasse zu geraten.

Die Russische Revolution war der bedeutendste politische Akt zu Beginn der Moderne. In der Architektur entfesselte sie himmelsstürmende Visionen und das weite Spektrum einer ekstatischen Ästhetik, von der die Architekten noch heute zehren. Damals war die Avantgarde davon überzeugt, daß sich die Welt nach ihren Ideen würde formen lassen und daß für die Architektur eine abenteuerliche Reise beginnen würde. Die Reise entwickelte sich zur Odyssee, und jede Architektengeneration erlebte ein ähnliches Wechselbad ästhetischer Hochgefühle und Depressionen.

Anfang der neunziger Jahre ist eine neue Generation auf der Suche nach dem Ursprung und Sinn ihrer geerbten Ästhetik genau dort angelangt, wo ihre Vorfahren die Reise begonnen haben: im Zeitalter der klassischen Moderne. Diese – heimliche – Renaissance erklärt eine neu entfachte Begeisterung für Le Corbusier, Leonidow und Lissitzky. Junge Architekten versuchen kongenial im Geiste der klassischen Moderne zu entwerfen und endlich das Ziel zu erreichen, das ihre Vorfahren nicht gefunden haben: die Vollendung der Moderne.

écologique du modernisme. Depuis le début de ce siècle, l'architecture d'une société technocratique menace aussi de tomber dans une impasse génétique.

La révolution russe a été le plus grand acte politique du début de l'époque moderne. Dans le domaine de l'architecture, elle a déclenché des visions démesurées et le large éventail d'une esthétique extatique dont les architectes vivent encore aujourd'hui. A cette époque, l'avant-garde était convaincue que le monde se laisserait former selon ses idées et qu'un voyage aventureux commencerait alors pour l'architecture. Le voyage s'est transformé en odyssée, et chaque génération d'architectes a fait l'expérience de ce genre d'alternance de délices et de dépressions esthétiques.

Au début des années 90, une nouvelle génération à la recherche de l'origine et du sens de l'esthétique héritée est parvenue exactement au point où ses ancêtres avaient commencé le voyage: à l'époque du modernisme classique. Cette renaissance – secrète – explique un enthousiasme à nouveau enflammé pour Le Corbusier, Leonidov et El Lissitzky. De jeunes architectes cherchent génialement à créer dans l'esprit du modernisme classique et à parvenir enfin au but que leurs ancêtres n'ont pas trouvé: la perfection du modernisme.

OSWALD MATHIAS UNGERS

Trade Fair Gate House, Frankfurt, 1983–1984

In Frankfurt in 1980 Ungers built Congress Hall 9 with the »Galleria«, followed in 1983 by the so-called Gate House. Its design is built upon three geometric elements: stone plinth, stone portal and glass shaft. In the mid-eighties, as the example of a rationalist »new clarity« in German architecture, the Gate House became a symbol of the trade fair city of Frankfurt.

1980 baute Ungers die Messehalle 9 mit der »Galleria« in Frankfurt, im Anschluß 1983 das sogenannte Torhaus. Das Entwurfskonzept fügt sich aus drei geometrischen Elementen zusammen: Steinsockel, Steintor und gläserner Schaft. Das Torhaus wurde Mitte der achtziger Jahre als Beispiel einer rationalistischen »Neuen Klarheit« in der deutschen Architektur zu einem Wahrzeichen für die Messestadt Frankfurt.

En 1980, Ungers construisit le hall 9 de la foire avec le »Galleria« à Francfort puis, en 1983, la dite maison-porche. Le projet est constitué de trois éléments géométriques: socle de pierre, porche de pierre et colonne de verre. Au milieu des années 80, la maison-porche est devenue, en tant qu'exemple de »nouvelle clarté« rationaliste dans l'architecture allemande, un symbole pour Francfort, ville des foires.

Architecture library in the architect's house in Cologne, 1989–1990

Between 1958 and 1959 Ungers built a house and office on his own plot of land in Köln-Mungersdorf. In 1990, in conjunction with various modifications and

extensions, he upgraded his home into a private miniature city. Art and nature were to be fused into an urban ensemble within the smallest possible space. The focal point of the whole became his private library, containing numerous first editions of European architectural treatises and theories, in which — according to Ungers — »the architectonic knowledge of our age is collected«. As the »Ungers Foundation for Architectural Studies«, the library is later intended for use by doctoral students, researchers and lecturers. Its design — a sunken cube — employs strict compositional orders such as the square and band grid, which are illustrated in the walls, floors and ceilings of the two-storeyed interior. Ungers employs brick and basalt from his native Eifel region as façade materials.

Auf seinem Privatgrundstück in Köln-Müngersdorf errichtete Ungers 1958 bis 1959 ein Wohnhaus mit Büro. 1990 rundete er im Zusammenhang mit verschiedenen Umbauten und Ergänzungen sein Wohnhaus zu einer privaten Miniaturstadt ab. Kunst und Natur sollten auf kleinstem Raum zu einem städtischen Ensemble verschmelzen. Mittelpunkt wurde seine Privatbibliothek mit zahlreichen Erstausgaben der europäischen Architekturlehren und -theorien, in der — so Ungers — »das architektonische Wissen unserer Zeit versammelt ist«. Die Bibliothek soll später als »Ungers-Stiftung für Architekturwissenschaft« Doktoranden, Forschern und Dozenten zu Studienzwecken dienen. Der Entwurf ist als eingesunkener Würfel auf strengen Ordnungen, wie Quadrat und Bandraster, aufgebaut, die sich im zweigeschossigen Innenraum an Wand, Boden und Decke abbilden. Als Fassadenmaterialien verwendete Ungers Ziegelstein und Basaltlava aus der heimatlichen Eifel.

En 1958/59, Ungers a construit une maison d'habitation avec bureau sur son terrain privé situé à Cologne-Müngersdorf. En 1990, il a complété sa maison au moyen de divers agrandissements et rajouts pour en faire une ville miniature privée. L'art et la nature devaient se fondre pour former un ensemble urbain sur un espace réduit. Le centre est devenu sa bibliothèque privée, qui comprend de nombreuses premières éditions des enseignements et théories architecturales européennes, et où »est rassemblée la science architectonique de notre époque«, dit Un-

gers. La bibliothèque doit servir ultérieurement aux études de candidats au doctorat, savants et professeurs comme »Fondation Ungers pour les sciences de l'architecture«. Le projet consiste en un cube affaissé, basé sur des ordres stricts tels que le carré et la bande modulaire qui se reproduisent dans l'intérieur à deux étages sur les murs, le sol et le plafond. Ungers employa la brique et la lave basaltique de sa Eifel natale comme matériaux de façade.

Opposite page: Fair Gate House, interior

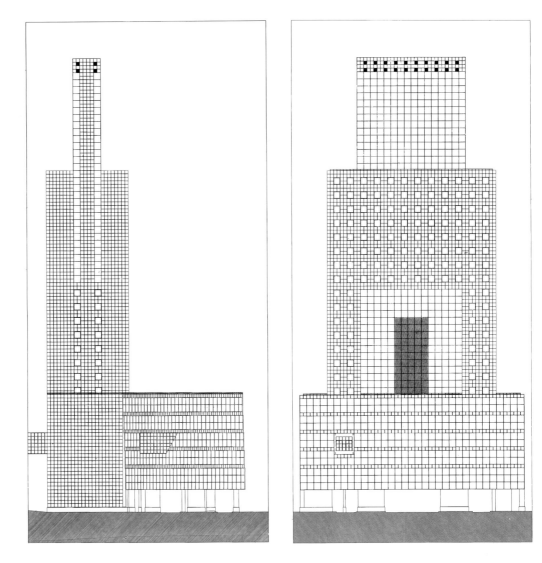

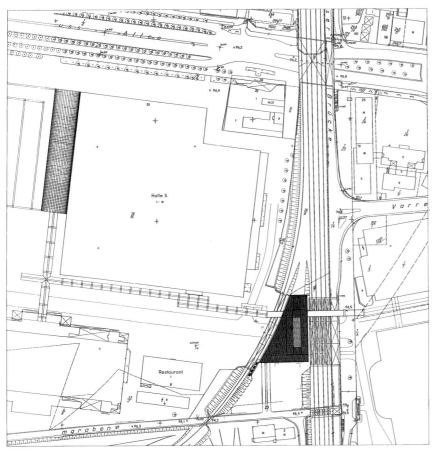

Fair Gate House, view from the west
(opposite page), elevations of north
side (left) and west side (right), site plan

The architect's library, street view and inner courtyard, sections, interior (opposite page)

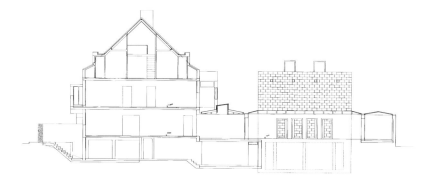

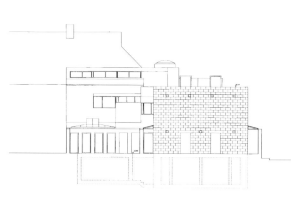

GOTTFRIED BÖHM

Bremerhaven University, 1982–1989

Up until the fifties, Bremerhaven was essentially characterized by small-scale building of three to four storeys. The design of the college takes up the same architectural proportions of the historical town centre. It is based upon a composition of gable-like structures with a round tower and glazed link sections. Its brick façades restate the characteristics and materials of existing buildings. A former brewery on the site was restored and incorporated into the design. The round tower contains an auditorium on the ground floor and rooms for students and lecturers above.

Bremerhaven war bis in die fünfziger Jahre kleinmaßstäblich, drei- bis viergeschossig bebaut. Der Entwurf für die Hochschule nimmt die architektonischen Proportionen der Altstadt wieder auf. Grundidee ist die Komposition giebelständiger Strukturen mit einem Rundturm und gläsernen Verbindungselementen. Die Ziegelfassaden setzen die Merkmale und Materialien vorhandener Bauten fort. Eine ehemalige Brauerei auf dem Grundstück wurde restauriert und in den Entwurf einbezogen. Der runde Turm enthält im Erdgeschoß ein Auditorium und darüber Räume für Studenten und Dozenten.

Jusque dans les années 50, la ville de Bremerhaven était composée de petites constructions de trois à quatre étages. Le projet pour l'université reprend les proportions architectoniques de la vieille ville. L'idée dominante est la composition de structures à pignon avec une tour ronde et des éléments de jonction en verre. Les façades en brique reproduisent les caractéristiques et les matériaux des constructions existantes. Une ancienne brasserie se trouvant sur le terrain a été restaurée et intégrée dans le projet. La tour ronde comprend une salle de conférences au rez-de-chaussée et des salles pour les étudiants et les professeurs au-dessus.

Conversion and restoration of Saarbrücken Palace, 1979–1989

Saarbrücken Palace dates back to a design by baroque architect Friedrich Joachim Stengel. The building originally comprised an emphatic central section and side wings in a horseshoe-shaped alignment. It burnt down in the nineteenth century, and subsequent re-building served to weaken its architectonic strength. The owner originally wished to reconstruct the central section true to its historical model. After restoration the Palace was intended to assume functions of the regional parliament. Its assembly chamber was also to serve for parties and concerts. Böhm built the central section to its historical proportions, but transformed it with modern architectural means into a glazed link between the historical side wings. He designed colourful ceiling decorations and murals for the assembly chamber.

Das Schloß Saarbrücken geht auf einen Entwurf des Barockbaumeisters Friedrich Joachim Stengel zurück. Ursprünglich hatte das Gebäude einen betonten Mittelbau und hufeisenförmig angeordnete Seitenflügel. Es brannte im 19. Jahrhundert aus und verlor durch verschiedene Umbauten seine architektonische Kraft. Der Bauherr wünschte zunächst eine Rekonstruktion des Mittelbaus nach historischem Vorbild. Nach der Restauration sollte das Schloß Funktionen des Landtags aufnehmen und der Plenarsaal zugleich für Feste und Konzerte nutzbar sein. Böhm realisierte den Mittelbau in historischen Proportionen, aber mit neuzeitlichen Architekturmitteln als gläsernes Bindeglied zwischen den historischen Seitenflügeln. Für den Plenarsaal entwarf er farbige Decken- und Wandgemälde.

Le château de Sarrebruck tire son origine d'un projet du bâtisseur baroque Friedrich Joachim Stengel. Au départ, le bâtiment comprenait un corps central dominant et des ailes en fer à cheval. Il brûla entièrement au XIXe siècle et perdit sa force architectonique à cause de diverses transformations. Le propriétaire souhaita d'abord que la partie principale soit reconstruite d'après le modèle historique. Après la restauration, le château devait faire office de parlement du land et la salle de l'assemblée devait également servir pour les fêtes et les concerts. Böhm a réalisé le bâtiment principal dans des proportions historiques mais avec des moyens architecturaux modernes, comme lien en verre entre les ailes historiques. Pour la salle de l'assemblée, il a conçu des fresques de plafond et des peintures murales.

University Library, Mannheim, 1986–1988

Böhm designed the library as an introverted architectural type, closed to the outside world, which unfolds around a hall. The building employs exposed concrete and an angled roof. The spherical objects ranked in front of the building were sculpted by Böhm himself. They portray a critical history of the city's typologies: the Gothic, baroque, modern Functionalist and chaotic city.

Böhm entwarf die Bibliothek als introvertierten, nach außen geschlossenen Architekturtypus, der sich um eine Halle entwickelt. Das Gebäude ist in Sichtbeton und mit geneigter Dachform gehalten, davor reihen sich kugelförmige Objekte auf, Arbeiten des Bildhauers Böhm. Sie stellen eine kritisch-historische Typologie der Stadt dar: die gotische, die barocke, die moderne funktionalistische, die chaotische Stadt.

Böhm conçut la bibliothèque comme type architectonique introverti, fermé vers l'extérieur, qui se développe autour d'un hall. Le bâtiment est fait de béton apparent et son toit est pentu. Des objets sphériques, œuvres du sculpteur Böhm, sont alignés devant le bâtiment. Ils représentent une typologie critique et historique de la ville: la ville gothique, la ville baroque, la ville fonctionnaliste moderne, la ville chaotique.

Opposite page: Bremerhaven University

Bremerhaven University, south façade,
roof plan, interior (opposite page)

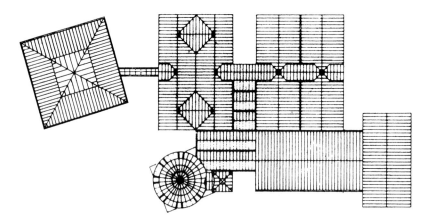

Saarbrücken Palace, view from the Schloßplatz with fountain in the foreground, ground plan, assembly chamber (opposite page)

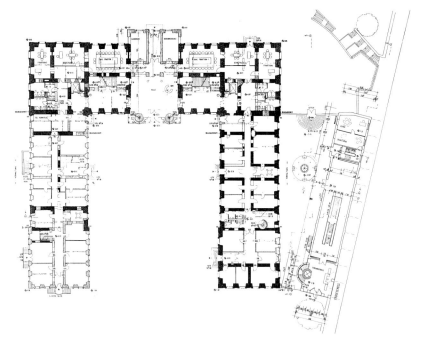

Mannheim University Library, elevation
sketches, stairways in the central hall,
spherical sculptures in the façade

Renault Distribution Centre, Swindon/Wiltshire, 1981–1983

The designer's brief was to develop a flexible and extended hall structure which would facilitate a large measure of prefabrication and could be built in a short space of time. All functional areas – distribution centre, computer centre, showroom, training centre and restaurant – totalling 10 000 m² are united under one roof. The construction grid measures 24 metres. The hall system is a significant prototype in the history of prefabricated suspension construction and has won numerous awards.

Die Entwurfsaufgabe bestand darin, eine flexible und weitgespannte Hallenstruktur zu entwickeln, die ein hohes Maß der Vorfertigung und kurze Bauzeiten ermöglichte. Alle Funktionsbereiche – Vertriebszentrale, Computerzentrum, Ausstellungsraum, technisches Ausbildungszentrum und Restaurant mit zusammen 10 000 Quadratmetern – sind unter einem Dach vereint. Das Konstruktionsraster beträgt 24 Meter. Das mehrfach ausgezeichnete Hallensystem ist ein bedeutender Prototyp in der Geschichte der Präfabrikation abgespannter Tragwerke.

Il s'agissait ici de développer une structure de hall variable, de vaste envergure, qui permette d'utiliser le plus possible de matériaux préfabriqués et soit rapide à construire. Tous les domaines fonctionnels – le centre de distribution, le centre informatique, la salle d'exposition, le centre de formation technique et le restaurant, en tout 10 000 mètres carrés – sont réunis sous un toit. Le module de construction mesure 24 mètres de côté. Ce système de halls, qui a remporté plusieurs prix, est un prototype important dans l'histoire de la préfabrication de structures porteuses haubanées.

Headquarters of the Hongkong and Shanghai Banking Corporation, Hong Kong, 1979–1986

Foster's main work offers an ideal illustration of his design aims: the portrayal of the skeleton and functional cores, prefabrication, and a maximum degree of flexibility of use. This last aspect proved particularly practical from the point of view of the bank's organisation, since permanent changes in organization made the ability to effect corresponding conversions necessary.

Das Hauptwerk Fosters zeigt seine Entwurfsziele in idealer Weise: die Inszenierung der Tragstruktur und der Funktionskerne, die Vorfertigung und ein Höchstmaß an Flexibilität der Nutzung. Gerade dieser Aspekt war für die Bankorganisation von praktischem Nutzen, da permanente Veränderung der Managementorganisation die Möglichkeit zu entsprechenden Umbauten erforderte.

La principale œuvre de Foster montre ses objectifs de manière idéale: réalisation de la structure porteuse et des noyaux fonctionnels, préfabrication et maximum de flexibilité de l'exploitation. Cet aspect fut justement utile à la banque dans la pratique, car les modifications permanentes de l'organisation du management exigeaient la nécessité des transformations adéquates.

Stansted Airport, near London, 1981–1991

London's third airport after Heathrow and Gatwick was designed by Foster. Glass membranes on tree-like megastructures span the two-storeyed airport on a band grid. The consistent division of function into two levels makes orientation considerably easier for flight passengers, who also enjoy an unhindered view of the runway. In developing and illustrating the complex supporting frameworks Foster made use of three-dimensional CAD programs, which provided an accurate spatial image of the finished architecture from the planning stage on.

Nach Heathrow und Gatwick entwarf Foster den dritten Flughafen für den Großraum London. Auf einem Bandraster überspannen gläserne Membranen auf baumartigen Megastrukturen den zweigeschossigen Flughafen. Die konsequente Funktionstrennung in zwei Ebenen bietet große Orientierungserleichterung für den Flughafengast, der in Stansted auch freien Blick auf das Rollfeld hat. Für die Entwicklung und Darstellung der komplexen Tragstrukturen setzte Foster CAD-Programme mit dreidimensionaler Darstellung ein, die schon im Planungsstadium eine genaue räumliche Vorstellung vom realisierten Zustand der Architektur ermöglichten.

Après Heathrow et Gatwick, Foster a conçu le troisième aéroport destiné au grand Londres. Sur une bande modulaire, des membranes de verre posées sur des mégastructures aux allures d'arbres recouvrent l'aéroport à deux étages. La séparation logique des fonctions sur deux niveaux donne des facilités d'orientation au voyageur qui a aussi une vue dégagée sur l'aire d'atterrissage et de décollage de Stansted. Pour la création et la représentation des structures porteuses complexes, Foster s'est servi de programmes CAD avec représentation tridimensionnelle, ce qui a permis de donner une idée spatiale exacte de l'architecture à réaliser dès le stade de la planification.

Opposite page: Renault Distribution Centre

Hongkong and Shanghai Bank, exterior
view, chairman's apartment at roof
level (above), detail in banking hall
(below)

Hongkong and Shanghai Bank, interior view of banking hall, ground plan at level 30

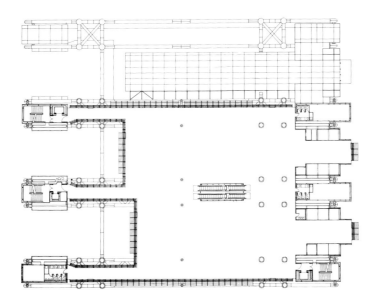

Following page: Stansted Airport

Stansted Airport, conceptual sketch,
views of concourse level and underground station, detail of structural tree
with skylight (opposite page)

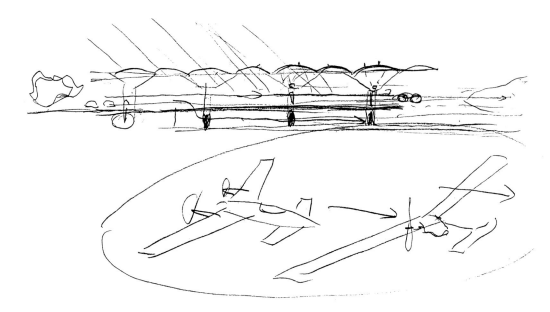

Extension to the State Gallery, Stuttgart, 1977–1984

In 1977, next to the classicist building of the old Staatsgalerie, Stirling and Wilford designed a museum of markedly urban, almost monumental character. Their building, the result of a competition, prompted a division in the architectural scene in Germany into two opposing camps: »Modernism versus Post-Modernism«.

Neben dem klassizistischen Bau der alten Staatsgalerie entwarfen Stirling und Wilford 1977 ein Museum mit ausgeprägter stadträumlicher, fast monumentaler Wirkung. Das Ergebnis des Wettbewerbs führte in Deutschland zu einer Spaltung der Architekturszene in gegnerische Lager: »Moderne versus Postmoderne«.

A côté du bâtiment néo-classique de l'ancienne Staatsgalerie, Stirling et Wilford ont conçu en 1977 un musée au caractère effet urbain marqué, presque monumental. En Allemagne, le résultat du concours a abouti à une scission de la scène architecturale en camps opposés: »modernisme contre postmodernisme«.

Clore Gallery, London, 1980–1986

The Clore Gallery represents a side-wing extension to the Tate Gallery. The design mediates between the old and the new through its surprising transformation of the façade materials of the older body of the Tate Gallery and the new building.

Die Clore Gallery erweitert die Londoner Tate Gallery um einen Seitenflügel. Der Entwurf vermittelt zwischen Alt und Neu durch eine überraschende Transformation der Fassadenmaterialien des älteren Teils der Tate Gallery und des neuen Gebäudes.

La Clore Gallery enrichit la Tate Gallery londonienne d'une aile. Le projet relie l'ancien et le nouveau grâce à une surprenante transformation des matériaux de la façade de l'ancienne partie de la Tate Gallery et du nouveau bâtiment.

Science Centre, Berlin, 1979–1988

The Science Centre houses the institutes of ecology, economic and social sciences. In their design, Stirling and Wilford successfully transform the spatial programme of a mono-functional office building into a composition of several buildings with a typological character: fortress, church, amphitheatre and campanile. This typological ensemble augments the existing historical lawcourt from the nineteenth century.

Das Zentrum umfaßt die Institute für Ökologie, Wirtschafts- und Sozialwissenschaften. Mit ihrem Entwurf für das Wissenschaftszentrum gelingt es Stirling und Wilford, das Raumprogramm eines monofunktionalen Bürogebäudes in eine Komposition mehrerer Gebäude mit typologischem Charakter zu verwandeln: Festung, Kirche, Amphitheater und Campanile. Dieses typologische Ensemble ergänzt das vorhandene historische Gerichtsgebäude aus dem 19. Jahrhundert.

Le centre comprend les instituts d'écologie, de sciences économiques et de sciences sociales. Avec leur projet pour le centre scientifique, Stirling et Wilford parviennent à transformer le programme des fonctions d'un immeuble de bureaux monofonctionnel en composition de plusieurs bâtiments avec caractère typologique: forteresse, église, amphithéâtre et campanile. Cet ensemble typologique complète le palais de justice historique du XIXe siècle.

Performing Arts Centre, Cornell University, Ithaca, New York, 1983–1988

The Performing Arts Centre complex houses teaching and practice rooms for the drama, dance and film departments as well as stages used for university performances. The various parts of the teaching building – proscenium theatre, flexible theatre and studios – are interconnected by a loggia, achieving harmony between the small town character and the wooded gorge. The three-storey entrance hall serves simultaneously as foyer for the proscenium and flexible theatres. The elevator tower rises high above the centre, signalling its presence from afar.

Der Gebäudekomplex des Performing Arts Centre beherbergt Unterrichts- und Übungsräume für die Abteilungen Schauspiel, Tanz und Film, dazu Bühnen für die Aufführungen der Universität. Die freie Komposition der Lehrgebäude mit Bühnentheater, flexiblem Theater und Studios wird von einer Loggia zusammengefaßt. Sie schafft den Übergang von der kleinen Idealstadt zum bewaldeten Taleinschnitt. Die dreigeschossige Eingangshalle ist gleichzeitig Foyer für Bühnentheater und flexibles Theater. Der Aufzugsturm ragt hoch über das Zentrum hinaus und signalisiert es von weitem.

Le bâtiment du Performing Arts Centre renferme des salles de cours et d'exercice pour les départements théâtre, danse et film, ainsi que des scènes pour les représentations de l'Université. Les bâtiments d'étude en composition libre, comprenant un théâtre à scène, un théâtre transformable et des studios, sont réunis par une loggia. Elle crée le passage entre la petite ville idéale et la vallée boisée. Le hall d'entrée de trois étages est le foyer du théâtre à scène et en même temps celui du théâtre transformable. La tour d'ascenseur s'élève au-dessus du centre et en signale la présence.

Opposite page: State Gallery Extension

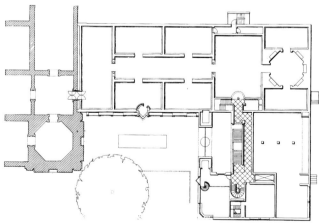

Clore Gallery, entrance, first floor plan,
perspective section through entrance
hall

Science Centre in Berlin, courtyard
(opposite page), view of companile,
second floor plan

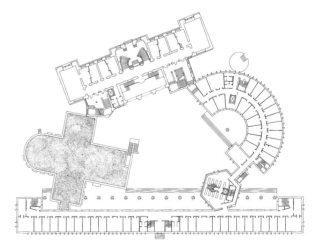

Cornell Performing Arts Centre, entrance (opposite page), overall view, plan

Patio Villa, Rotterdam, 1984—1988

The design is part of a semi-detached house and unfolds around an atrium on two storeys: a lower entrance and access level and an upper level facing the private garden. On the upper level, the kitchen and living room are grouped as a spatial continuum around the square inner courtyard. Bathroom, study and bedroom are screened off behind a long wall partition. The lower level contains the hall, garage and fitness room. The limited number of design elements employed results in a clarity of space in the tradition of Mies van der Rohe's country house projects.

Der Entwurf ist Teil eines Doppelhauses und entwickelt sich um ein Atrium auf zwei Ebenen: eine untere Eingangs- und Erschließungsebene und eine obere Ebene, die dem Privatgarten zugewandt ist. Im Obergeschoß gruppieren sich um den quadratischen Innenhof Küche und Wohnraum als räumliches Kontinuum. Bad, Arbeits- und Schlafzimmer sind durch eine lange Wandscheibe abgeschirmt. Im Untergeschoß liegen Diele, Garage und Fitneßraum. Die Beschränkung der Entwurfselemente führt zu einer Klarheit der Räume in der Linie der Landhausprojekte Mies van der Rohes.

Le projet fait partie d'une maison pour deux familles et se développe autour d'un atrium sur deux niveaux: un niveau inférieur pour l'entrée et un niveau supérieur tourné vers le jardin privé. A l'étage supérieur, la cuisine et la salle de séjour se regroupent autour de la cour intérieure carrée, comme continuum spatial. La salle de bain, le bureau et les chambres sont isolés par un long écran mural. A l'étage inférieur se trouvent le vestibule, le garage et la salle de culture physique. La limitation des éléments du projet entraîne une transparence des pièces dans la ligne des projets de villas de Mies van der Rohe.

Netherlands Dance Theatre, The Hague, 1984—1987

The Netherlands Dance Theatre stands surrounded by tall buildings in the centre of The Hague. It was originally planned as an extension to a circus theatre in Scheveningen. Its external architecture is colourful and dramatic, while its interior – despite its surprising impression of space – is functional and compact. The grid of supports of the underground car park thereby orders the free plan of the upper storeys. The stage measures 35 x 18 metres; the large auditorium has seating for 1001.

Im Zentrum von Den Haag, umringt von hohen Gebäuden, steht das Niederländische Tanztheater. Es war ursprünglich als Erweiterung eines Zirkus-Theaters in Scheveningen geplant. Von außen erscheint das Gebäude als farbenfrohe und dramatische Architektur. Im Inneren ist es trotz überraschender Raumwirkungen funktionell und kompakt entworfen. Dabei ordnet das Stützenraster der Tiefgarage die freie Grundrißentwicklung in den Obergeschossen. Die Bühne hat eine Größe von 35 x 18 Metern, der große Saal bietet 1001 Besuchern Platz.

Le théâtre de danse néerlandais se trouve au centre de La Haye, entouré de hauts bâtiments. A l'origine, il avait été prévu comme agrandissement d'un théâtre-cirque à Scheveningue. A l'extérieur, le bâtiment a un aspect très coloré et dramatique. A l'intérieur, il est conçu de manière fonctionnelle et compacte malgré des effets spatiaux surprenants. La grille modulaire du garage souterrain organise le plan libre aux étages supérieurs. La scène mesure 35 m x 18 m, la grande salle peut contenir 1001 spectateurs.

Centre for Art and Media Technology, Karlsruhe, project 1990

In the classicist city of Karlsruhe, Koolhaas has designed a futuristic centre for art and media technology on an ideal system of coordinates. His starting-point is the urban context of the railway station. His spatial and access solutions fuse station and museum into what is simultaneously a »railway-station museum« and »museum railway station«. The spatial structure of the building is surrounded by four zones enjoying a »futuristic potential«. Seen from the motorway, the centre may be perceived both as transparent architecture and »visual spectacle«.

Koolhaas entwarf in der klassizistischen Stadt Karlsruhe ein futuristisches Zentrum für Kunst und Medientechnologie auf einem idealen Koordinatensystem. Ausgangspunkt ist der städtische Kontext des Bahnhofsgeländes. Bahnhof und Museum überlagern sich in dem Er-

schließungs- und Raumkonzept zu einem »Bahnhofsmuseum« bzw. »Museumsbahnhof«. Die Raumstruktur des Gebäudes ist von vier Zonen umgeben, die über ein »futuristisches Potential« verfügen. Von der Autobahn her ist das Zentrum als transparente Architektur und »visuelles Spektakel« wahrnehmbar.

Koolhaas a conçu dans la ville néoclassique de Karlsruhe un centre futuriste pour l'art et la technologie des médias sur un système idéal de coordonnées. Le point de départ est le contexte urbain du terrain de la gare. La gare et le musée se superposent dans le concept d'entrée et d'espace intérieur pour former un »musée de la gare« ou bien une »gare du musée«. La structure spatiale du bâtiment est entourée de quatre zones qui disposent d'un »potentiel futuriste«. Depuis l'autoroute, le centre est perceptible en tant qu'architecture transparente et »spectacle visuel«.

Opposite page: Patio Villa

Netherlands Dance Theatre, entrance
and balcony in the foyer (opposite
page)

Centre for Art and Media Technology,
models of phase I (above) and II (below), CAD projection (opposite page)

The Paris Opera Dance School, Nanterre, 1983–1987

Planning for a ballet school for the Paris Opera began in 1983. After a two-year construction period, it was opened in 1987. Its spatial programme includes 10 ballet studios, an amphitheatre with seating for 300, a video library, a discotheque, the school administration offices and a boarding-school for 150 pupils with a restaurant. As in other of Portzamparc's designs, the architectural composition is developed using elements with thematic affinity to the building's function. Here, too, he succeeds in visualizing in his design the ballet school it serves.

1983 begann die Planung für die Tanzschule der Pariser Oper. Nach zweijähriger Bauzeit wurde sie 1987 eröffnet. Das Raumprogramm umfaßt 10 Tanzstudios, ein Amphitheater mit 300 Plätzen, eine Videothek, eine Diskothek, den Verwaltungsbereich für die Tanzschule und ein Internat für 150 Schüler mit Restaurant. Ähnlich wie bei anderen Entwürfen baut Portzamparcs Komposition der Baukörper auf Elementen auf, die eine thematische Affinität zur Bauaufgabe haben. So gelingt es ihm auch hier, die Zweckbestimmung der Tanzschule gestalterisch zu visualisieren.

La planification de l'Ecole de danse de l'Opéra de Paris a commencé en 1983. Après un délai de construction de deux ans, elle fut ouverte en 1987. Le programme d'aménagement spatial comprend dix studios de danse, un amphithéâtre de 300 places, une vidéothèque, une discothèque, le domaine administratif de l'Ecole de danse et un internat pour 150 élèves, avec restaurant. De même que dans d'autres pro-

jets, la composition des corps de logis de Portzamparc compte sur des éléments qui ont une affinité thématique avec la tâche à accomplir. Il parvient donc, ici aussi, à visualiser de manière créatrice la fonction de l'Ecole.

City of Music, west wing, Paris, 1984–1990

Portzamparc designed this new educational complex to replace the old College of Music. It lies at the southern entrance of the Park La Villette. Its spatial programme embraces a concert hall, 15 music rooms and more than 100 classrooms, as well as a music museum and 100 student apartments. The systematic decomposition of the overall form in the design clearly exposes the individual spatial components. In its variety of stereometric elements, cones, cubes, bands and prisms, Portzamparc's architectonic arrangement underlines his understanding of architecture as an art of movement.

Als Ersatz für die alte Musikhochschule entwarf Portzamparc diesen neuen Schulkomplex; er liegt am Südeingang vom Park La Villette. Das Raumprogramm umfaßt einen Konzertsaal, 15 Musiksäle und mehr als 100 Klassenzimmer. Darüber hinaus wurden ein Musikmuseum und l00 Wohnungen für Studenten errichtet. Die systematische Auflösung der Großform im Entwurf zeigt deutlich die einzelnen Bestandteile des Raumprogramms. In der Vielfalt der stereometrischen Elemente, Kegel, Würfel, Bänder, Prismen, unterstreicht das architektonische Arrangement Portzamparcs Auffassung von Architektur als Kunst der Bewegung.

Portzamparc a conçu ce nouveau complexe scolaire pour remplacer l'ancien conservatoire de musique; il se trouve au sud du Parc de La Villette. Le programme d'aménagement spatial comprend une salle de concert, 15 salles de musique et plus de 100 salles de classe. Il a en outre construit un musée de la musique et 100 appartements pour étudiants. La division systématique du grand format dans le projet montre nettement les composantes individuelles de l'aménagement spatial. Dans la diversité des éléments stéréométriques, cônes, cubes, bandes, prismes, l'arrangement architectonique souligne l'idée portzamparcienne de l'architecture en tant qu'art du mouvement.

Opposite page: The Paris Opera Dance School

City of Music, typical floor plan, view
from northwest, concert hall (opposite
page)

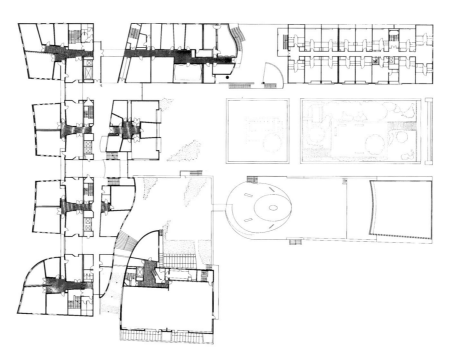

City of Music, view from southeast (opposite page), master plan, entrance hall

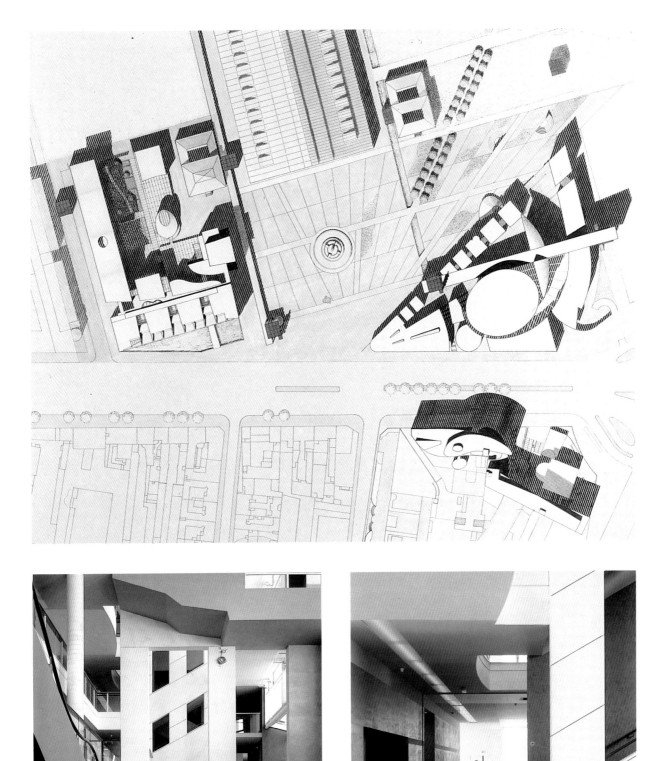

Il Palazzo Hotel, Fukuoka, Japan, 1987–1989 (with Morris Adjmi)

The hotel complex links the commercial district of Fukuoka with a proposed leisure and entertainment zone, of which the Il Palazzo hotel, rising seven storeys over its ground floor, represents an early stage. The monumental façade facing the river forms a striking new feature of the city skyline. The piazza in front of the entrance area is made an important architectonic feature. Typical for Rossi are the material and colour combinations created with the white-gold travertine of the piazza, the red marble-and-brick façade and the green steel mouldings.

Der Hotelkomplex verbindet das Geschäftsviertel von Fukuoka mit einer geplanten Erholungs- und Vergnügungszone. Einen Auftakt bildet das Hotel Il Palazzo, das sich siebenstöckig über einem Basisgeschoß erhebt. Die monumentale, flußzugewandte Fassade gibt dem Stadtbild ein neues Gepräge. Vor dem Eingangsbereich wird die ausgesparte Piazza zu einem wichtigen architektonischen Bestandteil. Der weißgoldene Travertin der Piazza bildet mit der roten Marmor- und Ziegelfassade und den grünen Stahlgesimsen eine für Rossi typische Material- und Farbkombination.

Le complexe hôtelier relie le quartier des affaires de Fukuoka à une zone de détente et de loisirs en projet. L'hôtel Il Palazzo, dont les sept étages s'élèvent au-dessus d'un étage de base, constitue un point de départ. La façade monumentale tournée vers le fleuve donne une nouvelle empreinte à la physionomie urbaine. Devant l'entrée, la piazza devient une composante architectonique essentielle. Le travertin blanc et or de la piazza constitue, avec la façade de marbre rouge et de brique et les corniches en acier vertes, une combinaison de matériaux et de couleurs typique de Rossi.

Carlo Felice New Theatre, Genoa, 1983–1991 (with Ignazio Gardella)

Genoa's Municipal Opera House was partly destroyed by bombing in 1943. The realization of Rossi's design represented the third — and at last successful — attempt to rebuild the theatre by the city authorities since the end of the war. A proposal for the theatre's renovation from 1969, as developed by Carlo Scarpa, was never executed. Rossi succeeded in integrating a tower-like structure into a sensitive urban context using the means of classical monumentality.

Das Städtische Opernhaus Genuas wurde 1943 durch Bombeneinwirkungen zum Teil zerstört. Die Realisierung von Rossis Entwurf ist der dritte, endlich geglückte Versuch der Stadtväter seit Ende des Krieges, den Wiederaufbau des Theaters voranzutreiben. 1969 hatte auch Carlo Scarpa einen Vorschlag zur Sanierung des Theaters entwickelt, der aber nicht zur Ausführung kam. Rossi gelang es, ein turmartiges Bauvolumen in einen empfindlichen Stadtkontext mit den Mitteln klassischer Monumentalität einzufügen.

L'Opéra de la ville de Gênes a été partiellement détruit par des bombes en 1943. La réalisation du projet de Rossi est le troisième essai enfin réussi, entrepris par les conseillers municipaux depuis la fin de la guerre pour activer la reconstruction du théâtre. En 1969 Carlo Scarpa avait également conçu une proposition de rénovation du théâtre qui ne fut toutefois pas réalisée. Rossi est parvenu à insérer un volume aux allures de tour dans un contexte urbain sensible avec les moyens de la monumentalité classique.

Opposite page: Il Palazzo Hotel

Il Palazzo Hotel, reception, north elevation

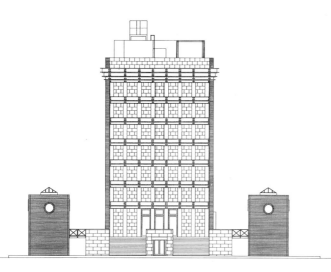

Il Palazzo Hotel, detail of west façade (above left), view from piazza to annex (above right), staircase in the annex (below left), El Dorado Bar (below right), first floor plan

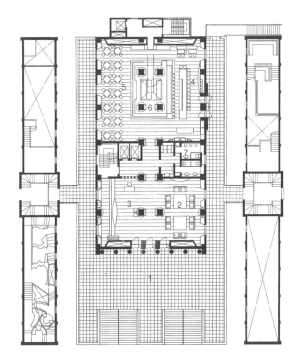

Carlo Felice Theatre, south-west elevation, auditorium, exterior view (opposite
page)

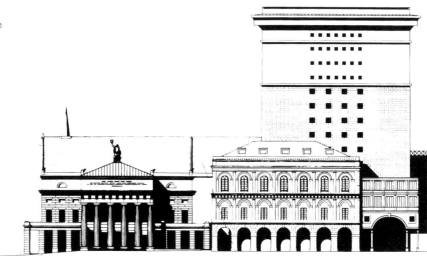

ENEA Research Centre, Rome, 1985

At the heart of the design is the tension created between shell and interior. Set against the high complexity of the installations inside the building is the modular reduction of the exterior façade, characterized by steel-grey prefabricated panels in a grid of 3.40 x 3.40 metres. Laboratories and offices are linked via balconies. The interior is dominated by two large halls separated by a glass corridor.

Der Entwurf lebt von der Spannung zwischen Hülle und Innenraum. Der hohen Komplexität der Installationen im Inneren des Gebäudes steht die modulare Reduktion der Fassaden gegenüber, die durch stahlgraue Fertigteilplatten auf einem Raster von 3,40 x 3,40 Metern geprägt sind. Labors und Bürobereiche sind durch Balkone miteinander verbunden. Der Innenraum ist von zwei großen Hallen bestimmt, die durch einen Glaskorridor getrennt sind.

Le projet vit de la tension entre l'enveloppe et l'intérieur. A la grande complexité des installations à l'intérieur du bâtiment s'oppose la réduction modulaire des façades marquées par des plaques faites d'éléments préfabriqués gris acier sur un module de 3,40 m x 3,40 m. Les laboratoires et les zones de bureaux sont liés les uns aux autres par des balcons. L'intérieur est déterminé par deux grands halls séparés par un corridor vitré.

University of Calabria, Cosenza, 1973–1985

Architecture as bridge with this principle in mind, Gregotti logically developed the university as a linear bridge structure in an animated environment. The university complex, comprising 21 departments, is over three kilometres long and is built upon a module measuring approx. 25 x 25 metres. The number of storeys devoted to each department varies between two and five, depending on topography. Two auditoriums are suspended within the bridge structure, but without obscuring the clarity of the megastructure.

Architektur als Brücke – dieser Grundidee seines Entwurfs folgend, entwickelte Gregotti die Hochschule konsequent als lineare Brückenstruktur in bewegtem Gelände. Der Universitätskomplex mit 21 Abteilungen ist über drei Kilometer lang und auf einem Modul von ca. 25 x 25 Metern aufgebaut. Die Geschossigkeit der Abteilungen variiert je nach Topographie zwischen zwei und fünf Stockwerken. In die Brückenstruktur sind auch zwei Hörsäle eingehängt, ohne die Transparenz der Megastruktur einzuschränken.

L'architecture comme pont – suivant cette idée fondamentale de son projet, Gregotti développa logiquement l'université en tant que structure-pont linéaire sur un terrain mouvementé. Le complexe universitaire, qui comprend 21 sections, mesure plus de trois kilomètres de long et est construit sur un module d'environ 25 m x 25 m. Le nombre d'étages des sections varie entre deux et cinq selon la topographie. Deux salles de conférences sont également suspendues dans la structure-pont sans limiter la transparence de la mégastructure.

Opposite page: ENEA Research Centre, entrance

ENEA Research Centre, view from
south, north-south section

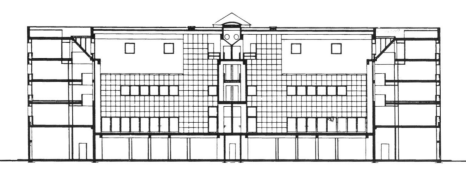

ENEA Research Centre, interior hall
with the connecting balcony on the right
side, east-west section

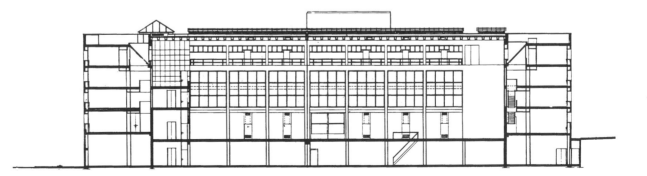

University of Calabria, construction details of pavilions and bridge, perspective drawing of the Crati valley

HANS HOLLEIN

Abteiberg Museum, Mönchengladbach, 1972–1982

The museum is built into the Abteiberg hillside. Its façades are executed in natural stone, aluminium, zinc and glass, corresponding in their variability to the multilayered spatial programme of the complex as a whole. As they pass through the galleries, visitors are presented with surprising vistas and a richly-varied succession of spatial situations with differentiated lighting conditions.

Das Museum ist in den Hang des Abteiberges hineingebaut. Die Fassaden sind aus Naturstein, Aluminium, Zink und Glas und entsprechen in ihrer Unterschiedlichkeit dem vielschichtigen Raumprogramm der Gesamtanlage. Überraschende Durchblicke und variantenreiche Raumsituationen mit differenzierten Lichtverhältnissen eröffnen sich dem Besucher auf seinem Rundgang.

Le musée est niché dans la pente de l'Abteiberg. Les façades sont construites en pierres naturelles, aluminium, zinc et verre, et correspondent dans leur diversité au programme d'aménagement spatial de toute l'installation. De surprenantes percées et des situations variées aux luminosités différenciées s'ouvrent au visiteur en train de faire le tour de l'exposition.

Haas Building, Vienna, 1985–1990

As a prominent architectural feature opposite St Stephen's Cathedral, the Haas department store represents a contribution to the reconstruction of Stock-im-Eisen-Platz. Above its four-storeyed hall, extravagant in both details and materials, rise two office and banking floors and – overlooking the square in a glass cylinder – a two-storeyed restaurant.

Als stadträumliche Figur gegenüber dem Stephansdom soll das Haas-Kaufhaus einen Beitrag zur Rekonstruktion des Stock-im-Eisen-Platzes leisten. Über der viergeschossigen, in Details und Material verschwenderisch gestalteten Halle des Kaufhauses befinden sich zwei Büro- und Banketagen und – dem Platz zugewandt, in einem Glaszylinder – ein zweigeschossiges Restaurant.

Le magasin Haas doit fournir sa contribution à la reconstruction de la place Stock-im-Eisen en tant que figure urbaine vis-à-vis de la cathédrale Saint-Etienne. Deux étages de bureaux et de banque et un restaurant à deux étages – tourné vers la place, dans un cylindre de verre – se trouvent au-dessus du hall de ce magasin sur quatre étages construit avec prodigalité pour ce qui est des détails et des matériaux.

Museum of Modern Art, Frankfurt, 1982–1991

From an extremely limiting site in the shape of an acute-angled circle segment, Hollein developed a logical architectural form: a »slice of cake«, with its tip designed as a sculpture. The interior is characterized by a flight of steps running diagonally from the uppermost museum level down to the main entrance. Variable spaces are grouped around the central exhibition hall.

Aus einer extrem begrenzten Grundstückssituation, einem spitzwinkligen Kreissegment, entwickelte Hollein eine folgerichtige Architekturform: ein »Tortenstück«, dessen Spitze als Skulptur ausgebildet ist. Der Innenraum ist von einer Treppenkaskade bestimmt, die vom obersten Niveau des Museums diagonal bis zum Haupteingang verläuft. Um die zentrale Ausstellungshalle herum gruppieren sich variable Flächen.

A partir d'un terrain extrêmement limité, un segment de cercle à angle aigu, Hollein a développé une forme architectonique conséquente: une »part de gâteau« dont la pointe a la forme d'une sculpture. L'intérieur est déterminé par une cascade d'escaliers qui descend en diagonale du niveau supérieur du musée jusqu'à l'entrée principale. Des surfaces variables se groupent autour du principal hall d'exposition.

Museum in the Rock, Salzburg, project 1990

The idea of situating a museum in the hollowed-out rocks of the Mönchsberg was developed to enable the projected art museum to be built right next to the old city centre of Salzburg. While the natural, hewn rock surface can be seen in the central area, other rooms, particularly those housing the collections, are fitted with a second, neutral inner shell. Changing amounts of daylight allowed in through a crowning flat dome and various shafts topped with glass pavilions heighten the sculptural effect of this »excavated« building.

Um ein geplantes Kunstmuseum in unmittelbarer Nähe zur Altstadt Salzburgs bauen zu können, entstand die Idee, dieses in den plastisch ausgehöhlten Felsen des Mönchsberges zu legen. Während die zentraleren Raumbereiche dabei die natürliche, abgescherte Felsoberfläche zeigen, sind vor allem die Sammlungsräume mit einer zweiten, neutralen Innenschale versehen. Wechselnder Tageslichteinfall durch eine krönende flache Kuppel und diverse Schächte mit aufgesetzten Glaspavillons erhöhen die skulpturale Wirkung des »subtraktiv« erstellten Bauwerks.

Pour bâtir le musée prévu dans le voisinage immédiat de la vieille ville de Salzbourg, où les constructions sont très resserrées, on a eu l'idée de le nicher dans la roche excavée plastiquement du Mönchsberg. Alors que les salles centrales montrent la surface naturelle, cisaillée, de la roche, d'autres salles, surtout les salles de collections, sont pourvues d'un second revêtement intérieur neutre. Les rayons changeants de la lumière du jour passant à travers la coupole plate qui couronne le bâtiment et différents puits coiffés de pavillons de verre, rehaussent le caractère sculptural du bâtiment construit de manière »soustractive«.

Opposite page: Abteiberg Museum, interior

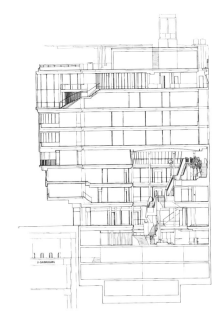

Haas Building, section and interior views of shopping area

Haas Building with St. Stephen's
Cathedral, ground floor plan

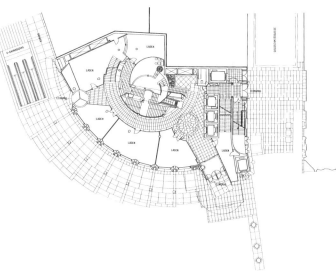

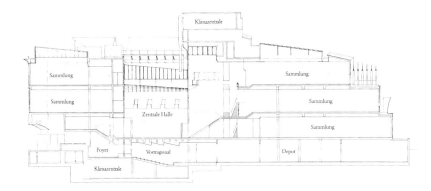

Museum in the Rock, model, section

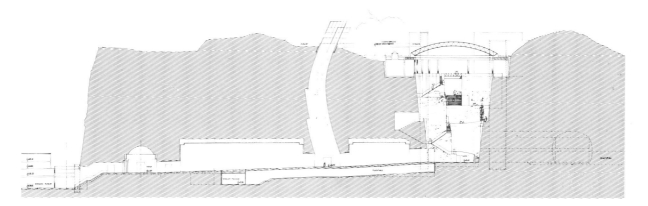

GUSTAV PEICHL

Phosphate Elimination Plant, Berlin, 1980–1985

Its plan is inspired by the desire to marry functional programme with artistic design, and operating procedures thus determine both layout and architectural form. The pump house and its accompanying transformer station, built to prespecified dimensions in the north of the complex, are thereby assigned to the functional centre, namely the mixing tower in the middle of the circular purification tanks. The overall shape of the control building suggests the image of a ship – an expressive machine aesthetic typical for Peichl.

Grundidee des Entwurfs ist die Integration der technisch-funktionellen Konzeption und der architektonischen Gestaltung: Die Betriebsabläufe bestimmen die Grundrißlösung und gleichzeitig die Architekturform des Entwurfs. Das Pumpenhaus und die zugeordnete Trafostation sind nach vorgegebenen Dimensionen im Norden der Anlage dem Funktionsmittelpunkt, dem Mischturm inmitten der kreisförmigen Flockerbecken, zugeordnet. Die Großform des Betriebsgebäudes vermittelt das Bild eines Schiffes – in einer für Peichl typischen expressiven Maschinenästhetik.

L'idée de base du projet est l'intégration de la conception technico-fonctionnelle et de la réalisation architectonique: le déroulement opérationnel détermine le plan ainsi que la forme architectonique du projet. Le bâtiment des pompes et la station de transformation coordonnée sont attribuées, selon des dimensions données, au centre de fonction au nord du terrain, à la tour de mixage au milieu du bassin de floculation circulaire. Le grand format du bâtiment d'exploitation donne l'image d'un bateau – dans une expressive esthétique de la machine typique de Peichl.

Burgenland Regional Studio for Austrian State Radio (ORF), Eisenstadt, 1981–1983

Burgenland regional studio for Austrian State Radio is the sixth to be built to the same overall architectural plan. Its layout is dominated by a central hall ringed by five production departments – TV studio, public studio, sound broadcasting studio, control room and office wing. The architecture of this complex in

the open countryside reflects Peichl's aim to create a harmonious dialogue between a self-confident machine aesthetic as world of art on the one hand, and nature on the other.

Das Landesstudio Burgenland des Österreichischen Rundfunks war das sechste, das nach dem gleichen architektonischen Konzept gebaut wurde. Der Grundriß ist durch eine zentrale Halle bestimmt, an die sich ringförmig die fünf Bereiche der Produktion anschließen: Fernsehstudio, Publikumsstudio, Hörfunkstudio, Kontrollraum und der Bürotrakt. Die Architektur in der freien Landschaft verdeutlicht Peichls Intention einer spannungsvollen Harmonie von selbstbewußter Maschinenästhetik als Kunstwelt auf der einen und Natur auf der anderen Seite.

Le studio du Burgenland pour la radio autrichienne fut le sixième à avoir été construit d'après le même concept architectonique. Le plan est déterminé par un hall central auquel se rattachent circulairement les cinq domaines de la production: studio de télévision, studio du public, studio de la radio, salle de contrôle et aile de bureaux. L'architecture placée dans le paysage découvert illustre l'intention de Peichl: créer une harmonie riche en tensions entre l'esthétique hardie de la machine en tant que monde artistique d'une part et la nature d'autre part.

Extension to the Städel Museum, Frankfurt, 1987–1990

The three-storeyed addition is linked to the main neo-Classical building via a bridge on the first floor. In the foyer of the main entrance Peichl quotes – in almost Post-Modernist manner – architectural motifs of the School of Vienna. A flexible ground floor offers space for changing exhibitions. A film and lecture theatre is located in the basement. In its height and proportions Peichl's building complements its older counterpart. It is clad – quietly and modestly – in white natural stone and roofed with copper.

Der dreigeschossige Erweiterungsbau schließt mit einer Verbindungsbrücke im ersten Obergeschoß an den neoklassizistischen Altbau an. Im Foyer des Haupteingangs zitiert Peichl – fast in postmoderner Manier – Architekturmotive der Wiener Schule. Das flexible Erdgeschoß bietet Flächen für Wechsel-

ausstellungen, im Untergeschoß befindet sich ein Film- und Vortragssaal. Der Bau nimmt in Höhen und Proportionen Rücksicht auf den bestehenden Baukörper und ist – ruhig und zurückhaltend – mit weißem Naturstein verkleidet, das Dach in Kupfer gedeckt.

L'annexe de trois étages est rattachée au vieux bâtiment néo-classique par un pont de jonction situé au premier étage. Dans le foyer de l'entrée principale, Peichl cite – d'une manière presque postmoderne – des motifs architectoniques de l'Ecole viennoise. Le rez-de-chaussée flexible offre des surfaces pour les expositions temporaires; une salle de projection et de conférences se trouve au sous-sol. Dans sa hauteur et dans ses proportions, la construction tient compte des corps de bâtiment existants et est – tranquille et discrète – revêtue de pierre naturelle blanche, tandis que le toit est recouvert de cuivre.

Opposite page: Phosphate Elimination Plant

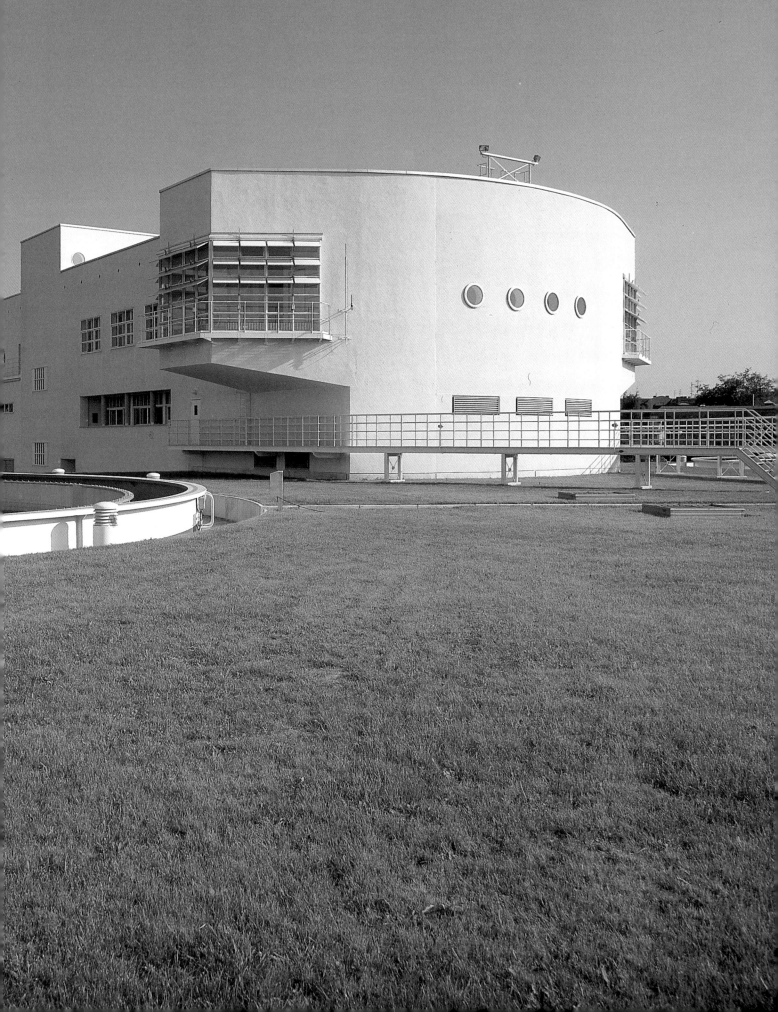

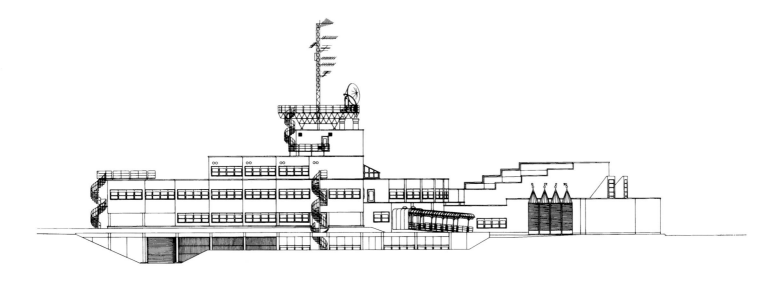

Burgenland Regional Broadcasting
Studio, foyer, conceptual sketch

Following page: Städel Museum
Extension

Städel Museum Extension, foyer (above
and opposite page), conceptual sketch
of museum access

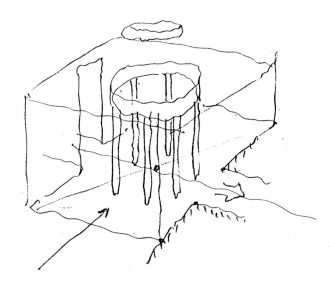

Funder Factory Works 3 in St. Veit/Glan, Kärnten, 1988–1989

It was intended that the architecture of this paper-coating factory should be as symbolic as it was unmistakable. The design is based on the principle of adding sculpturally-modelled functional elements to the production hall. The rotation and angling of individual architectural components thereby undermines visual conventions in order to create identity. The hall, deliberately kept white and free of detail, is differentiated by the playful use of »dancing stacks« which conclude the power station, the »media bridge« connecting the power and production areas and the free design of the winged roof.

Eine Papierbeschichtungsfabrik sollte als zeichenhafte und unverwechselbare Architektur entworfen werden. Das Entwurfskonzept basiert auf der Idee, einer Produktionshalle plastisch gestaltete Funktionselemente anzulagern. Um Identität zu schaffen, werden durch Verdrehung und Verkippung einzelner Architekturelemente tradierte Sehgewohnheiten in Frage gestellt. Der spielerisch-plastische Abschluß der Energiezentrale mit »tanzenden Kaminen«, die »Medienbrücke« als Verbindung von Energie- und Produktionsbereich und die freie Gestaltung des aufgebogenen Flugdaches differenzieren die bewußt weiß und detaillos gehaltene Halle.

Une usine à enduire le papier devait être conçue comme architecture symbolique et originale. Le projet se base sur l'idée consistant à rattacher des éléments fonctionnels plastiques à un hall de production. Pour créer une identité, des habitudes visuelles traditionnelles sont remises en question en tordant et

en faisant basculer des éléments architecturaux. La bordure légèrement en relief de la centrale énergétique avec des »cheminées dansantes«, le »pont des médias« comme lien entre le domaine énergétique et le domaine de production ainsi que la conception libre de l'avant-toit cambré différencient le hall volontairement blanc et dépourvu de détails.

Roof conversion for Falkestrasse 6, Vienna, 1983–1988

A lawyer's firm in a historical district of Vienna required extension by means of a roof conversion. The design shows visualized energy lines which, coming from the street below, span the project and explode and open up the existing roof. The notion of »deconstruction« is here made visible in its most literal sense. Surfaces of open glazing and closed folds control the light reaching the two-storeyed conversion.

Eine Rechtsanwaltskanzlei in einem historischen Viertel Wiens sollte durch einen Dachgeschoßausbau erweitert werden. Der Entwurf zeigt visualisierte Entwurfslinien, die – von der Straße ausgehend – das Projekt überspannen und das bestehende Dach zerbrechen und öffnen. Die Idee der »Dekonstruktion« wird hier im wahrsten Sinne des Wortes sichtbar. Offene, verglaste und geschlossene, gefaltete Flächen der Hülle kontrollieren das Licht in dem zweigeschossigen Projekt.

Une étude d'avocat située dans un quartier historique de Vienne devait être agrandie en aménageant les combles. Le projet montre des lignes visualisées qui – partant de la rue – recouvrent le projet, brisent et ouvrent le toit existant. L'idée de la »déconstruction« devient ici visible dans toute l'acception du terme. Dans ce projet sur deux étages, les surfaces ouvertes et vitrées, fermées et pliées de l'enveloppe contrôlent la lumière.

Ronacher Theatre, Vienna, project 1987

With a design brief requiring a non-optimally functioning theatre from the last century to be converted into a functioning theatre for the next century, the architects felt it necessary to considerably broaden the public experience of a theatre with proscenium stage. Their

design proposes a »publicization« of the main and subsidiary theatres by emphasizing the multi-functionality of their spaces, as well as providing a roof terrace with open-air stage, restaurants, bars and a public video library. The Ronacher is thereby understood not simply as a theatre, but as a vast »cultural export media machine«.

Um ein nicht optimal funktionierendes Theater aus dem vorigen Jahrhundert in ein funktionierendes Theater für das nächste Jahrhundert umzubauen – so die Entwurfsaufgabe –, schien es den Architekten geboten, den Erlebnisraum des Publikums gegenüber einem Theater mit Guckkastenbühne deutlich zu erweitern. Ihr Konzept sieht eine »Veröffentlichung« der Haupt- und Nebenbühnen durch die Multifunktionalität der Räume vor, eine Dachterrasse mit einer Freiluftbühne, Restaurants, Bars und eine öffentliche Videothek. Das Ronacher wird dabei nicht nur als Theaterhaus verstanden, sondern als eine riesige »Kulturexport-Medien-Maschine«.

Pour transformer un théâtre du siècle passé ne fonctionnant pas de façon optimale en théâtre fonctionnant bien pour le siècle prochain – telle était la tâche –, il parut nécessaire aux architectes d'agrandir nettement l'espace où le public participe au spectacle, par rapport à un théâtre avec scène fermée par un rideau. Leur idée prévoit une »ouverture« de la scène principale et des scènes secondaires grâce au multifonctionnalisme des salles, une toiture en terrasse avec scène en plein air, des restaurants, des bars et une vidéothèque publique. Le Ronacher est non seulement assimilé à un théâtre, mais aussi à une »machine géante à exportations culturelles et à médias«.

Opposite page: Funder Factory

Funder Factory, glass corner (opposite page), side entrance, isometric drawing

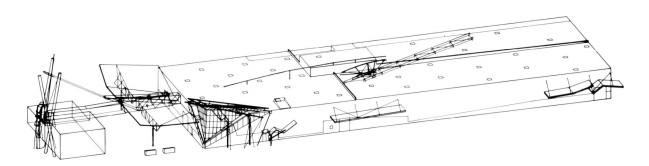

Falkestraße roof conversion, overall
view and floor plan

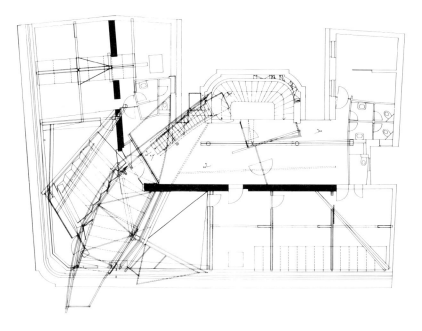

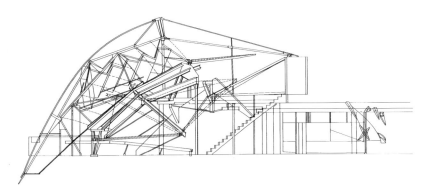

Falkestraße roof conversion, elevation,
details and interior views

  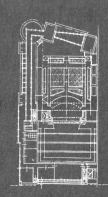 

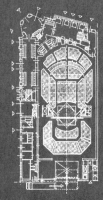 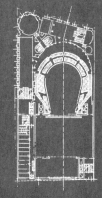 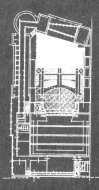 

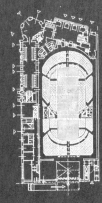 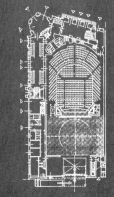 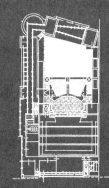 

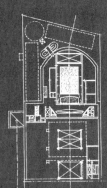 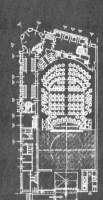 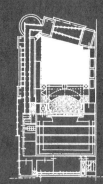 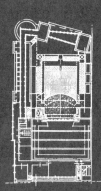

Ronacher Theatre project, model, conceptual sketch, plan with auditorium variations (opposite page)

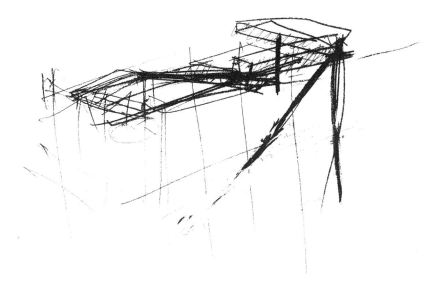

Villa Escarrer, Palma de Mallorca, 1985–1988

Villa Escarrer, with a living area of approx. 300 m², treads a delicate line between modernism and tradition. It starts from a modular concept developed from Palladio's villa »La Malcontenta«, whereby its pure basic form has been overlaid and modified by the design aims of flexibility and growth on the one hand and the local topography of the site on the other. The contemporaneous reconstruction of Mies's Pavilion in Barcelona prompted an increased sensitivity in terms of materials employed.

Die Villa Escarrer mit einer Wohnfläche von ca. 300 m² entstand im Spannungsfeld von Moderne und Tradition. Ausgangspunkt ist ein modulares Konzept, das auf Palladios Villa »La Malcontenta« aufbaut. Die Entwurfsziele Flexibilität und Wachstum einerseits und die Topographie des Geländes andererseits haben die reine Grundfigur überlagert und verändert. Die zeitgleiche Rekonstruktion des Miesschen Pavillons in Barcelona führte zu einer gesteigerten Sensibilität für die verwendeten Materialien.

La villa Escarrer, qui a une surface habitable d'environ 300 m², a été créée dans le cadre du modernisme et de la tradition. Le point de départ est un concept modulaire basé sur la villa »La Malcontenta« de Palladio. La flexibilité et la croissance visées d'une part et la topographie du terrain d'autre part ont recouvert et transformé la figure fondamentale pure. La reconstruction parallèle du pavillon de Barcelone de Mies a entraîné une sensibilité accrue pour les matériaux employés.

Die Wohnanlage mit 200 Appartements ist ein Projekt im Rahmen des sozialen Wohnungsbaus. Der Entwurf ist durch verschiedene, einzeln stehende Gebäude bestimmt, die einen städtischen Wohnblock von ca. 100 x 100 Metern Seitenlänge ergeben. Der öffentliche Wohnhof im Inneren des Blocks mit Sichtverbindungen und Fußwegen zu den peripheren Straßenräumen ist urban entworfen. In dieser kommunikativen Idee steckt eine soziale Grundhaltung des Entwurfs, die als richtungsweisend gelten darf.

La zone résidentielle, qui comporte 200 appartements, est un projet réalisé dans le cadre de l'habitat à loyer modéré. Le projet est déterminé par divers bâtiments isolés qui donnent un îlot urbain de maisons d'environ 100 m x 100 m. La cour publique, qui est située au centre du pâté de maisons et est liée visuellement et par des chemins pour piétons aux rues qui l'entourent, est conçue de manière urbaniste. Cette idée communicative recèle une attitude sociale fondamentale du projet que l'on peut considérer comme pleine d'avenir.

Mollet City Block, Barcelona, 1983–1987

This residential complex of 200 apartments is a public-housing project. The design is characterized by various detached buildings which together compose a residential block measuring approx. 100 x 100 metres. The sensitively-designed public courtyard inside the block offers visual links and footpaths to the peripheral street spaces. The communicative concept of the complex reflects an underlying social design philosophy of a pioneering nature.

Opposite page: Villa Escarrer, pergola

Villa Escarrer, garden view, swimming
pool, living room, entrance, section and
hall (opposite page)

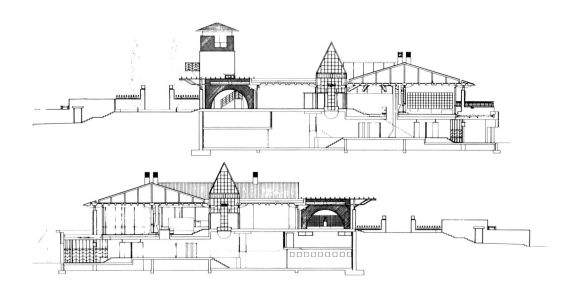

Mollet City Block, overall view and plan

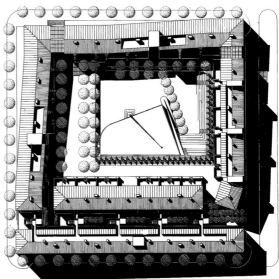

Mollet City Block, details

JOSE RAFAEL MONEO

Museum of Roman Art, Merida, 1980–1985

Merida, called the »Spanish Rome«, was one of the most important outposts of the Roman Empire on the Iberian peninsula. Archaeological excavations were begun at the end of the nineteenth century, in the course of which significant findings were made. Moneo's museum, built over an excavation site containing the remains of a Roman settlement, respects the tradition of Roman architecture, whereby it creates a dialectic tension between the archaeological findings and the dominating walls of the new building. The constructive mastery of brick masonry can be seen in the consistent development of the overall structure.

Merida, das »Spanische Rom« genannt, gehörte zu den wichtigsten Städten des römischen Reiches auf der iberischen Halbinsel. Ende des 19. Jahrhunderts begannen archäologische Ausgrabungen, bei denen bedeutende Funde gemacht wurden. Über dem Grabungsfeld mit Resten einer römischen Siedlung errichtete Moneo das Museum in der Tradition der römischen Baukunst. Dabei stehen die archäologischen Fundstücke in einer spannungsvollen Dialektik zu den dominierenden Wandscheiben des Neubaus. Die konstruktive Beherrschung des Ziegelmauerwerks zeigt sich in der konsequenten Durchbildung des gesamten Bauwerks.

Mérida, appelée la »Rome espagnole«, faisait partie des principales villes de l'empire romain sur la presqu'île ibérique. A la fin du XIXe siècle, on procéda à des fouilles archéologiques pendant lesquelles d'importantes découvertes furent faites. Moneo a construit le musée dans la tradition de l'architecture romaine sur le champ de fouilles qui recèle les restes d'une cité romaine. Les objets archéologiques trouvés sont placés de manière intéressante par rapport aux murs dominants du nouveau bâtiment. La maîtrise constructive de la muraille de briques se montre dans la formation logique de l'ensemble de la construction.

Previsión Española Building, Seville, 1982–1987

This insurance building in the immediate vicinity of the »Torre del Oro« takes up the architectural traditions of its historical neighbourhood and renounces sugared means of self-portrayal. In its architectural elements and proportions, the building merges harmoniously into its environment without thereby sacrificing its own identity. Alongside the restraint of its overall form, the masterly details and sensitive composition of its materials of brick, marble and steel are particularly striking.

Das Versicherungsgebäude in unmittelbarer Nachbarschaft des »Torre del Oro« nimmt die Bautradition der historischen Umgebung auf und verzichtet auf überzogene Mittel der Selbstdarstellung. Das Gebäude fügt sich in seinen Architekturelementen und Proportionen harmonisch in den Kontext ein, ohne auf einen eigenen Ausdruck zu verzichten. Neben der Zurückhaltung der Großform fallen die meisterhaften Details und die feinsinnige Komposition der Materialien auf, Ziegel, Marmor und Stahl.

Le bâtiment de la compagnie d'assurances, qui se trouve à proximité immédiate de la »Torre del Oro«, reprend la tradition architecturale du milieu historique et renonce aux moyens excessifs de l'auto-représentation. Dans ses éléments architecturaux et dans ses proportions, le bâtiment s'intègre harmonieusement dans le contexte sans renoncer à une expression personnelle. Outre la discrétion du grand format, on remarque les détails magistraux et la subtile composition des matériaux, brique, marbre et acier.

Bank of Spain, Jaen, 1983–1988

This two-storeyed bank building is placed within a protective courtyard setting, thereby creating a self-contained urban ensemble which goes beyond symbolic and practical considerations of security. The generously-proportioned entrance area with its shady canopy roof underlines the public character of the bank. Moneo emphasizes the plastic quality of the building with his materials of brick and exposed concrete. The typographical legend and emblem of the bank appear surprisingly as decoration and stylistic return to the vocabulary of Spanish traditionalism of the thirties.

Ein zweigeschossiges Bankgebäude ist in eine schützende Hofanlage eingestellt. Über den symbolischen und praktischen Sicherheitsaspekt hinaus entsteht so ein eigenständiges städtebauliches Ensemble. Der großzügig angelegte Eingangsbereich mit einem schattenspendenden Vordach unterstreicht den öffentlichen Charakter der Bank. Moneo arbeitet die plastische Wirkung des Gebäudes mit den Materialien Ziegel und Sichtbeton heraus. Die typographische Inschrift und das Emblem der Bank werden überraschend als Ornament inszeniert – ein stilistischer Rückgriff auf das Repertoire des spanischen Traditionalismus der dreißiger Jahre.

Un bâtiment de banque à deux étages est placé dans une cour protectrice. Au-delà de l'aspect de la sécurité symbolique et pratique, un ensemble urbain autonome est ainsi créé. La vaste zone d'entrée avec auvent faisant de l'ombre souligne le caractère public de la banque. Moneo met en relief l'effet plastique du bâtiment avec les matériaux brique et béton apparent. De façon inattendue, l'inscription typographique et l'emblème de la banque sont employés comme ornements – un recours stylistique au répertoire du traditionalisme espagnol des années 30.

Opposite page: Museum of Roman Art

Museum of Roman Art, ground floor
with excavations (opposite page),
street view, section

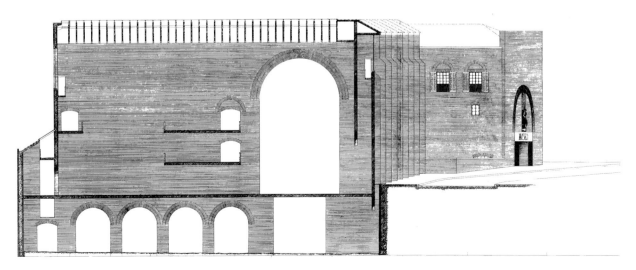

Previsión Española Building, view in city context, elevation

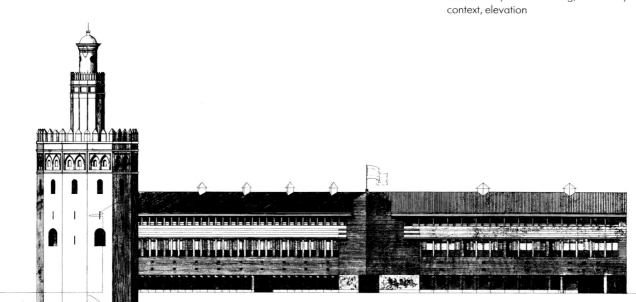

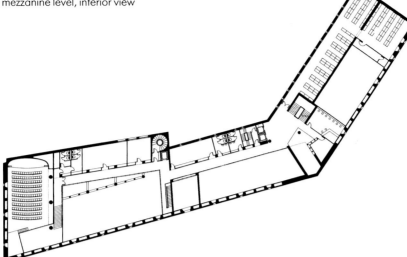

Previsión Española Building, plan of
mezzanine level, interior view

Bank of Spain in Jaen, street view (opposite page), lighting detail, elevation of entrance side

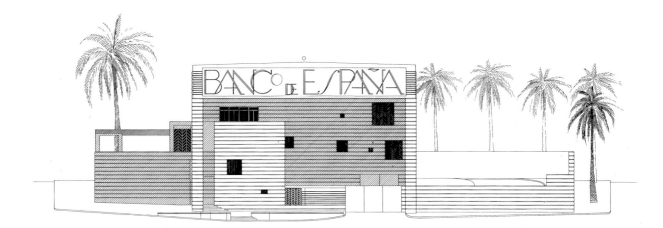

INDEX

CREDITS

Arcaid, Richard Bryant 24, 26, 27, 28, 89, 90/91, 92, 93, 94, 95
Archipress, Foto Stephane Couturier 32
AVEC Audiovisual 54
Basilico, Gabriele 34, 39, 114, 115
Bednorz, Achim 2, 14, 47
Biggi, Dida 154, 155, 156, 157
Bildarchiv Foto Marburg 49
Borel, Nicolas 104, 106, 108, 109 u.
Casals, Lluís 60, 61, 145, 146, 147, 148, 149
Cook, Peter 22
Couturier, Stephane 105
Deutsches Architekturmuseum 16, 42
Dissing & Weitling 52
Engel, W. Willi 62
Esto, Foto Peter Aaron 97, 98/99, 100, 101
Foster Associates, Foto Andrew Ward 80
Foster Associates, Foto Richard Davies 81
Foster Associates, Foto Ian Lambot 82, 83
Frahm, Klaus 12, 19, 25, 30, 44, 45, 58, 59, 151, 152, 153
Freíxa, Ferran 64
Fürst, Peter H. 72
FWG, Georg Riha 123, 124, 125
Goebel, Wilhelm 56
Gössel, Peter 36
Gregotti, Vittorio 117, 118, 119, 120, 121
Hollein, Hans 127
Kirkwood, Ken 84/85, 86, 87
Koolhaas, Rem 96, 102, 103
Kruse, Ingrid von 122
Leistner, Dieter 18, 48, 67, 68, 70, 71, 73, 74, 75, 76, 77, 78, 78/79, 126
Martorell, Bohigas, Mackay 144
Maurer, Paul 33
Mebusch, Heinz-Günter 66
Moneo, Rafael 150
Monthiers, Jean-Marie 107
Nacása & Partners 111, 112, 113
Nikolic, Monika 132/133, 134, 135
Pedersen, Poul 53
Peichl, Gustav 128
Pinkster & Tahl 8, 9
Portzamparc, Christian de 109 o.
Rau, Uwe 38, 116
Rossi, Aldo 40
Schaewen, Deidi von 35
Schafler, Ali 129, 130, 131
Schmölz, Karl Hugo 20
Simonetti, Filippo 46
Stirling, James & Michael Wilford Associates 88
Syndication, Gert von Bassewitz 10
Syndication, Bent Rej 55
Ullstein Bilderdienst 110
Zugmann, Gerald 50, 136, 137, 138, 139, 140, 141, 143